Praise for
The President's House

"Truman brings readers inside the White House, taking them on a notably reverential tour of its storied history, its well-known architecture, and its intricate behind-the-scenes workings."

—*Publishers Weekly*

"Charming and sometimes entrancing."
—*St. Louis Post-Dispatch*

"Never dry or dull, the energetic narrative brings the history of this almost mythical residence to life."
—*Booklist*

"Wonderfully written by a former First Daughter."
—North Carolina *Pilot*

By Margaret Truman

Souvenir
White House Pets
Harry S Truman
Women of Courage
Letters from Father:
The Truman Family's Personal Correspondences
Bess W. Truman
Where the Buck Stops
First Ladies
The President's House: 1800 to the Present
The Life of a White House Girl

IN THE CAPITAL CRIMES NOVELS
Murder in the White House
Murder on Capitol Hill
Murder in the Supreme Court
Murder in the Smithsonian
Murder on Embassy Row
Murder at the FBI
Murder in Georgetown
Murder in the CIA
Murder at the Kennedy Center
Murder at the National Cathedral
Murder at the Pentagon
Murder on the Potomac
Murder at the National Gallery
Murder in the House
Murder at the Watergate
Murder at the Library of Congress
Murder in Foggy Bottom
Murder in Havana
Murder at Ford's Theatre
Murder at Union Station
Murder at the Washington Tribune
Murder at the Opera
Murder on K Street
Murder Inside the Beltway
Monument to Murder

THE
PRESIDENT'S
HOUSE

THE PRESIDENT'S HOUSE

1800 TO THE PRESENT

The Secrets and History of
the World's Most Famous Home

MARGARET TRUMAN

Ballantine Books • New York

In memory of my mother and father

Contents

	Acknowledgments	xi
	Presidents and Their Wives	xiii
1	Magic and Mystery in a Unique Place	3
2	From Palace to Mansion to Powerhouse	17
3	The President's Park	35
4	History Happened Here	49
5	Working the House	65
6	Womanpower	83
7	The West Wing	97
8	Frontstairs, Backstairs	115
9	Bed, Breakfast, and Beyond	133
10	Growing Up Under Glass	151
11	Here Come the Brides	171
12	Talking Dogs and Other Unnatural Curiosities	191
13	Minding the Media	211
14	Keeping Killers and Kooks at Bay	229
15	The People's White House	247
16	The White House Forever	263
	Index	265

Acknowledgments

A BOOK LIKE this can only come to life with the help of many people. I hope no one thinks I learned all these fascinating facts and stories about the White House simply by hanging around the place in my twenties! High on my gratitude list is Scott Roley, assistant director of the Harry S Truman Presidential Library, who shared with me oral histories of several of the leading players in my father's administration. At least as much appreciation goes to my old friend Pauline Testerman, the Truman Library's audiovisual archivist, who supplied me with many of the pictures that appear in these pages. An equally warm thank you to the White House Historical Association, in particular Bill Bushong, Maria Downs, and photo archivist Harmony Haskins. Barbara McMillan of the White House Curator's Office and Candace Shyreman, assistant curator of Blair House, were always generous and enthusiastic. The John F. Kennedy and Franklin D. Roosevelt presidential libraries were also notably cooperative, as was the dedicated staff of the Library of Congress. Of crucial importance was—and is—my editor, Samuel S. Vaughan, whose wise counsel and knowledge of American history kept me on the right track in matters both small and large. Finally, I would like to thank Tom and Alice Fleming for their advice and insights during the research and organization of this book.

Presidents and Their Wives

☆ George Washington
Martha Dandridge Custis
Washington
April 30, 1789–March 3, 1797

☆ John Adams
Abigail Smith Adams
March 4, 1797–March 3, 1801

☆ Thomas Jefferson
Martha Wayles Skelton
Jefferson
March 4, 1801–March 3, 1809

☆ James Madison
Dolley Payne Todd Madison
March 4, 1809–March 3, 1817

☆ James Monroe
Elizabeth Kortright Monroe
March 4, 1817–March 3, 1825

☆ John Quincy Adams
Louisa Catherine Johnson
Adams
March 4, 1825–March 3, 1829

☆ Andrew Jackson
Rachel Donelson Robards
Jackson
March 4, 1829–March 3, 1837

☆ Martin Van Buren
Hannah Hoes Van Buren
March 4, 1837–March 3, 1841

☆ William Henry Harrison
Anna Symmes Harrison
March 4, 1841–April 4, 1841

☆ John Tyler
Letitia Christian Tyler
Julia Gardiner Tyler
April 6, 1841–March 3, 1845

☆ James K. Polk
Sarah Childress Polk
March 4, 1845–March 3, 1849

☆ Zachary Taylor
Margaret Smith Taylor
March 4, 1849–July 9, 1850

☆ Millard Fillmore
Abigail Powers Fillmore
Caroline Carmichael
McIntosh Fillmore
July 10, 1850–March 3, 1853

☆ Franklin Pierce
Jane Appleton Pierce
March 4, 1853–March 3, 1857

☆ James Buchanan
March 4, 1857–March 3, 1861

☆ Abraham Lincoln
Mary Todd Lincoln
March 4, 1861–April 15, 1865

☆ **Andrew Johnson**
Eliza McCardle Johnson
April 15, 1865–March 3, 1869

☆ **Ulysses S. Grant**
Julia Dent Grant
March 4, 1869–March 3, 1877

☆ **Rutherford B. Hayes**
Lucy Webb Hayes
March 4, 1877–March 3, 1881

☆ **James A. Garfield**
Lucretia Rudolph Garfield
March 4, 1881–September 19, 1881

☆ **Chester A. Arthur**
Ellen Herndon Arthur
September 20, 1881–March 3, 1885

☆ **Grover Cleveland**
Frances Folsom Cleveland
March 4, 1885–March 3, 1889

☆ **Benjamin Harrison**
Caroline Scott Harrison
Mary Lord Dimmick
Harrison
March 4, 1889–March 3, 1893

☆ **Grover Cleveland**
Frances Folsom Cleveland
March 4, 1893–March 3, 1897

☆ **William McKinley**
Ida Saxton McKinley
March 4, 1897–September 14, 1901

☆ **Theodore Roosevelt**
Alice Lee Roosevelt
Edith Carow Roosevelt
September 14, 1901–March 3, 1909

☆ **William Howard Taft**
Helen Herron Taft
March 4, 1909–March 3, 1913

☆ **Woodrow Wilson**
Ellen Axson Wilson
Edith Bolling Galt Wilson
March 4, 1913–March 3, 1921

☆ **Warren G. Harding**
Florence Kling De Wolfe
Harding
March 4, 1921–August 2, 1923

☆ **Calvin Coolidge**
Grace Goodhue Coolidge
August 3, 1923–March 3, 1929

☆ **Herbert Hoover**
Lou Henry Hoover
March 4, 1929–March 3, 1933

☆ **Franklin D. Roosevelt**
Anna Eleanor Roosevelt
Roosevelt
March 4, 1933–April 12, 1945

☆ **Harry S Truman**
Elizabeth Wallace Truman
April 12, 1945–January 20, 1953

☆ Dwight D. Eisenhower
Mamie Doud Eisenhower
January 20, 1953–January 20,
1961

☆ John F. Kennedy
Jacqueline Bouvier Kennedy
January 20, 1961–November
22, 1963

☆ Lyndon B. Johnson
*Claudia (Lady Bird) Taylor
Johnson*
November 22, 1963–January
20, 1969

☆ Richard M. Nixon
Patricia Ryan Nixon
January 20, 1969–August 9,
1974

☆ Gerald Ford
*Elizabeth Bloomer Warren
Ford*
August 9, 1974–January
20, 1977

☆ Jimmy Carter
Rosalynn Smith Carter
January 20, 1977–January 20,
1981

☆ Ronald Reagan
*Jane Wyman Reagan
Nancy Davis Reagan*
January 20, 1981–January 20,
1989

☆ George H. W. Bush
Barbara Pierce Bush
January 20, 1989–January 20,
1993

☆ William J. Clinton
Hillary Rodham Clinton
January 20, 1993–January 20,
2001

☆ George W. Bush
Laura Welch Bush
January 20, 2001–

THE
PRESIDENT'S
HOUSE

The South Portico at twilight. I've always thought that the White House looks particularly magical in the glow of early evening. Credit: White House Historical Association

Magic and Mystery in a Unique Place

THE LAST TIME I was in Washington, D.C., I walked by the White House on the way to dinner at a nearby restaurant. Hidden floodlights made the historic building glow like a mansion in a vision or a dream. Suddenly I thought: *I am not the woman who lived in that house more than fifty years ago. She is a completely different person. I barely know her.*

The words whispered in my mind like a voice from another world. I was remembering, or trying to remember, what it meant to be the daughter of the president of the United States, living in that shining shimmering house. The one inescapable thing I recalled was the difference. I have lived in several houses and apartments, and spent some time in splendid establishments, including a few royal palaces. But not one of them—nor all of them together—can compare to the feeling I recalled from my White House days.

That was when I resolved to write this book about one of the most mysterious, terrifying, exalting, dangerous, fascinating houses in the world. I think everyone who has ever lived there would agree that it's a special experience—a unique combination of history, tragedy, comedy, melodrama, and the ups and downs of ordinary living, all under one roof.

II

Men bearing that unique title, president of the United States, the office my father called "the greatest in the history of the world," have paced the White House's darkened halls in periods of national crisis.

In the basement and attic rooms are the memories of the hundreds of other people who lived a large part of their working lives in this unique house. Some, I regret to say, were slaves. But the house, paradoxical as always, gradually became a place where free African-Americans demonstrated their right to equality.

Maggie Rogers began working as a White House maid when William Howard Taft became president in 1909. Her daughter, Lillian Rogers Parks, was hired as a seamstress at the White House in 1929 and worked there until the end of the Eisenhower administration in 1961. Growing up, Lillian once asked her mother if she would be happier (and better paid) at some millionaire's mansion elsewhere in the capital. Maggie Rogers scorned the idea. "Heavens no, child! Be it ever so elegant, there's no place like the White House. Why, I'm living history!" There was black pride and White House pride achieving a magical fusion.

Also worth commemorating are the efforts of the dedicated and courageous men who have struggled to keep presidents and their families alive. We know them now as members of the Secret Service. But their predecessors are equally memorable, standing guard at the White House's doors in loose-fitting suits that concealed their pistols.

Few people know about the many acts of kindness these protectors perform for presidents and first ladies. Perhaps the most touching story comes from the sad days of President Woodrow Wilson's decline in 1919. Felled by a stroke, he sank into near despair as Congress rejected his dream of world peace embodied in the League of Nations.

When the crippled president went for a ride in the afternoon, the Secret Service used to round up a small crowd of government employees and strolling tourists, who waited at the White House gate to cheer him when he returned. It was a testament to how much these men cared about the president.

III

Among the most intriguing White House denizens are the men and women who have worked beside presidents as their spokespersons or confidential advisers. For many of them, the experience was more than a little harrowing—and in a few cases, fatal.

I am thinking of one of my most heartbreaking White House memories—the death of my father's boyhood friend and press secretary, Charlie Ross. Charlie went through high school with Harry Truman and went on to become a top-ranked Washington, D.C., reporter for the *St. Louis Post-Dispatch*. When my father turned to him for help in 1945, Charlie gave up a comfortable salary and rational hours for the ordeal of a White House in which clocks and sensible schedules ceased to exist. Five exhausting years later, Charlie Ross collapsed and died of a heart attack at his desk. A weeping Harry Truman said the country had lost a great public servant—and he had lost his best friend.

IV

That memory leads us to another cadre of White House inhabitants, although many presidents and their families might be reluctant to bestow that title on them: the men and women of the media. They, too, participate in the aura of the White House—to the point that they sometimes act as if they run the place.

My favorite White House media story comes from my friend President Gerald Ford. Jerry says he and veteran newswoman Helen Thomas were strolling on a street near the White House when he saw one of those old-fashioned scales that gave you your fortune and weight for a penny. Jerry read the little fortune card aloud: "You are a marvelous orator and leader of men. Your future in your chosen career could not be brighter."

Helen, looking over his shoulder, said: "It's got your weight wrong, too."

As the wife (now widow) of a newspaperman, I recognize the necessity for such irreverence. As the daughter of a president, I don't have to like it. But I am prepared to include it, somewhat ruefully, in the White House's story.

V

The White House is far more than the place where presidents and hundreds of staffers work and presidential families live. It is also the place where America's pride and dignity are displayed. At official dinners and receptions, when the president enters the room to the U.S. Marine Band's resounding "Hail to the Chief," people recognize not only a powerful man but the nation, the United States of America. The immense amount of time and effort that is devoted to entertaining visitors from around the country and the world is a fascinating and important story. It, too, is part of the White House aura.

What a roster these visitors constitute! They range from the king and queen of England, whose snobbish servants started an uncivil war with the White House staff, to Russian grand dukes and Japanese noblemen, from world renowned politicians such as Winston Churchill, who gave himself a mild heart attack trying to open his bedroom window, to Cherokee and Creek and Sioux Indian chiefs, who did war dances on the lawn. Marvelous musicians such as pianist Vladimir Horowitz, soprano Jessye Norman, and cellist Pablo Casals have filled presidential ears with beautiful music. Entertainers such as Frank Sinatra and Barbra Streisand have made the place sound, for a few hours, like Broadway. Thick-necked political bosses have more than once converted the president's second-floor study or the Oval Office into smoke-filled rooms, where political careers were empowered—or destroyed.

VI

Admission to the White House has never been restricted solely to the elite. From the earliest days, presidents recognized its symbolic importance as a place where they greeted anyone and everyone who wanted to come in the door. Several of these early receptions turned into mob scenes that threatened to ruin the rugs and wreck the furniture—and even made one or two chief executives fear for their lives.

Presidents and their staffs soon learned they had to set limits to White House access if they wanted to have time to conduct the nation's business. But the tradition of the White House as the people's house lived on—and is alive and well in contemporary Washington.

You used to be able to stroll by 1600 Pennsylvania Avenue any day you chose, and see a long line of tourists—some of the million and a half Americans who streamed through the first-floor public rooms each year. As a small *d* as well as a large *D* democrat, that statistic has always gladdened my heart. Visiting the White House in person is a little like meeting a celebrity face-to-face. You get impressions and feelings that a newspaper or TV show—or even this book—can't communicate. After the terrorist attacks of September 11, 2001, and during the war with Iraq in the spring of 2003, tours were temporarily suspended because of concerns about security. Group tours, which have to be arranged in advance, were eventually reinstated. I hope it won't be too much longer before the tours for the general public will also be resumed.

VII

The idea that the White House is the people's house has caused fierce quarrels every time a president or first lady tried to change the building in any significant way. John Quincy Adams was denounced for buying a billiard table. Millard Fillmore was attacked for putting in a bathtub.

Grace Coolidge caused an uproar when she tried to redecorate the family quarters with furniture in the style of the period in which the White House was built. Ironically, Jacqueline Kennedy did the same thing for the public rooms some thirty-eight years later and was wildly acclaimed for her efforts. When my father added a balcony to the South Portico, you would have sworn from the screams that impeachment was just around the corner.

Then there are the media and congressional snipers who are ready to open fire if they detect the slightest hint of snobbery or pretentiousness in the president's lifestyle. Their salvos were largely responsible for depriving at least one president, Martin Van Buren, of a second term in the White House.

Van Buren had served as Andrew Jackson's vice president, which all by itself made him a ripe target for the Whigs (forerunners of the Republicans) who were against anyone or anything connected with Jackson. On top of that, Van Buren liked to live, dress, and entertain in style, which made it easy to cast him as a decadent aristocrat.

In the spring of 1840, a few months before Van Buren began his campaign for reelection, the House of Representatives was considering a bill to allot funds for landscaping the grounds and repairing the furniture in the President's House. Whig congressman Charles Ogle of Pennsylvania took advantage of the occasion to launch a passionate attack against Van Buren. Taking his listeners on an imaginary tour of the "Presidential Palace," Ogle commented on its "regal splendor." He condemned the president's bonbon stands and green glass finger bowls and assailed him for serving fancy French food instead of such old-fashioned favorites as "hog and hominy" or "fried meat and gravy."

Ogle's harangue went on for three days and included more than a few comments about the down-home virtues of the Whig presidential candidate, William Henry Harrison. The oration kicked off one of the most vitriolic campaigns in American history, and sent Martin Van Buren home to New York.

Van Buren's ordeal may have been on Franklin D. Roosevelt's mind when he was planning a state dinner for the king and queen of England during their visit to the United States in 1939. FDR wanted to serve a typical American dish, terrapin à la Maryland, as the first course, but maître d'hôtel Alonzo Fields informed him that the White House had no terrapin dishes.

Fields took advantage of the opportunity to mention that the White House's gold flatware was missing some crucial pieces. There were no soup spoons or fish knives, and the salad forks had to be washed between courses so they could double as dessert forks.

FDR was sympathetic. "But you know," he told Fields, "if we were to ask for all those things you say we need, the politicians would make headlines out of the gold tableware being bought for the White House."

Although Roosevelt was too astute a politician to go for the gold, he did manage to squeeze a set of terrapin dishes into the White House budget.

VIII

For anyone living or working in the White House, or visiting it, or merely touring the place, everything seems larger than life. One reason for this effect is factual: The house is ten times larger than your ordinary dwelling and considerably larger than most mansions. George Washington, the man who saw the future greatness of America when it was a mere collection of quarrelsome former colonies, insisted on building it that way.

History is another reason for the White House's aura: It virtually oozes from the walls. You find it impossible to forget you are walking halls and climbing stairs where Thomas Jefferson and Abraham Lincoln and Theodore Roosevelt trod before you.

No one put the mystical side of the White House more succinctly than President Grover Cleveland. A big, bulky, blunt-talking lawyer from Buffalo, New York, he seemed the last man in the world to notice such things. But after a few months in the White House, he told a friend: "Sometimes I wake at night . . . and rub my eyes and wonder if it is not all a dream." If someone as commonsensical as Cleveland could be spooked, what chance do ordinary mortals have in the grip of this special atmosphere?

IX

My father, another commonsensical man, was convinced that the old house was haunted. Let me give you an excerpt from a letter he wrote to my mother.

Night before last I went to bed at nine o'clock after shutting my doors. At four o'clock I was awakened by three distinct knocks on my bedroom door. I jumped up and put on my bathrobe, opened the door, and no one was there. Went out and looked up and down the hall, looked into your room and Margie's. Still no one there. Went back to bed after locking the doors and there were footsteps in your room whose door I'd left open. Jumped up and looked and no one there! Damn place is haunted sure as shootin'. Secret Service said not even a watchman was up here at that hour.

I told Dad, "You better lock your door and prop up some chairs and next time you hear knocks, don't answer. It may be Andrew Jackson in person!"

Lillian Rogers Parks, working in the small room in the northwest corner of the house (later my bedroom), next to a larger room where Lincoln's bed and other furniture were at that time, heard footsteps approaching the door between the two rooms. Every time she opened it, there was no one there. She asked the houseman on duty why he was walking back and forth in that room without coming in the door.

"I just came on duty," he informed her. "That was Abe you heard."

He was "perfectly serious," Mrs. Parks added.

X

One reason for the disorienting effect of the White House is the incredible power it emanates. That alone can induce strange behavior in men and women. The day after my father became president, he summoned his old friend, business executive Eddie McKim, to the Oval Office to discuss the possibility of a job in his administration. Dad and Eddie had been in the army together during World War I. They had been close friends for twenty-five or thirty years. Yet when Eddie stepped into the Oval Office, a kind of mental and emotional paralysis seized him. He kept calling Dad "Mr. President" and stood at virtual attention before the big desk.

Dad told Eddie to call him "Harry"—and sit down. "I can't do that Har . . . Mr. President," Eddie said. Reluctantly, Dad decided it might be better if Eddie supported the Truman administration as a private citizen.

An opposite variation on the effect of power on personality is a syndrome my father christened "Potomac fever." Its main symptom is a ballooning self-importance that runs roughshod over anyone and anything in its way. PF can and does afflict almost everyone in the Washington, D.C., power structure, but it is especially prevalent in the White House. The mere ability to get on the telephone and say "This is the White House calling" is enough to make anyone's judgment go squishy.

The White House as a power center is by no means all bad. Presidents need power to get things done and the White House is one of their strongest assets. My favorite story in this department is a little gathering Lyndon Johnson hosted at

1600 Pennsylvania Avenue for a group of congressmen who had been voting against him much too often. "Nice place, isn't it?" LBJ said. "Take a good look around. If you guys don't change your votin' habits, it's the last time you'll see it while I'm president."

XI

More than one president has told me that on his last day in the White House, he walked through all the rooms on the first floor, from the East Room to the State Dining Room, remembering moments of pride and pleasure. The harrowing memories—Dad once wrote to his mother that he barely had time to eat his meals as he raced from crisis to crisis—fade away. What remains is the central meaning of the White House and the unique satisfaction of winning a place in its history.

If I had to put that meaning into one word, I would choose *glory*. I don't think even the most cynical newspaper or TV reporter, who knows the worst failings of presidents and first ladies, would deny that in the long run, glory is what the White House is all about. Everyone who has ever lived or worked there has a piece of the glory of this vanguard nation, the United States of America. Even for those who found more unhappiness than happiness in the White House, the glory is still there—a consolation and a reward.

Questions for Discussion

1. Why is living in the White House a special experience?

2. What are some of the ways in which a close connection to the White House might affect people?

3. What makes the White House different from other public buildings?

This 1807 print is the earliest known picture of the White House. You have to study it closely to realize it's the same building. Credit: White House Historical Association (The White House Collection)

From Palace to Mansion
to Powerhouse

THE WHITE HOUSE has 132 rooms, 32 bathrooms, 5 full-time chefs, a tennis court, a jogging track, a movie theater, a billiard room, infrared electric sensors that can detect any movement on the grounds, a SWAT team standing by on the roof every time the president enters or leaves the building, a digitalized locator box that tracks each member of the first family anywhere in the world, and a Situation Room that can monitor troop movements by satellite, retrieve reports electronically from key government agencies, and otherwise deal with almost every conceivable crisis in our terror-ridden modern world.

Two centuries separate this high-tech house from the building that Pierre Charles L'Enfant, the French engineer and architect, designed in 1791 while simultaneously laying out the plans for Washington, D.C. L'Enfant envisioned a palace about five times the size of today's White House standing in an eighty-acre President's Park complete with terraces, fountains, and formal gardens.

II

President George Washington believed that L'Enfant's design would lend dignity and importance to the new government. Not everyone in his administration agreed. A new political party, the Democratic-Republicans, led by Thomas Jefferson, considered the palace a monstrosity that might inspire its occupants to behave like royalty. L'Enfant's concept proved to be short-lived for reasons more personal than political. The Frenchman managed to alienate everyone he worked with, including George Washington, and he soon found himself unemployed.

A competition was held to find a new architect for what was now being called the President's House. The winner was a Charleston, South Carolina, man, Irish-born James Hoban. Among the losers was a gifted amateur architect, Thomas Jefferson, who had submitted his design under the pseudonym A.Z.

Hoban's building was smaller and plainer than L'Enfant's palace. Washington requested that it be made larger and grander. He also wanted it built of stone but the cost was prohibitive, so the inner walls were made of brick. The outer walls were sandstone, which had to be whitewashed to keep out the moisture. Before long, people were calling the place the White House.

III

George Washington, who had been so involved in the design of the President's House, never got to live in it. On November 1, 1800, his successor, John Adams, became its first occupant. The day after his arrival, Adams wrote to his wife, Abigail: "I pray Heaven to bestow the best of blessings on this house, and on all that shall hereafter inhabit it. May none but honest and wise men ever rule under this roof."

Abigail Adams, who arrived two weeks later, may have shared his sentiments, but she was not oblivious to the shortcomings of their official home. About half of the thirty-six rooms were still unplastered and only six were fit to live in. Abigail found the house cold and dark and so large, it would take thirty servants to run it. In a letter to her daughter, she wrote: "the great unfinished audience-room, I make a drying-room of, to hang up the clothes in."

IV

As a Democratic-Republican, John Adams's successor, Thomas Jefferson, might have been expected to refuse to live in the President's House. Although Jefferson described the house as "big enough for two emperors, one pope and the grand lama," he not only moved in, he set to work to make the place more habitable. His first order of business was removing the wooden privy that stood beside the house in full view of passersby. It was replaced by two water closets (toilets) installed at each end of the second floor.

Jefferson also commissioned the construction of wings on the east and west sides of the mansion to house the president's coaches, servants' quarters, and other important but not necessarily attractive areas. The wings were one-story extensions connected by colonnades to the basement of the White House, which was at ground level.

The President's House took another step closer to becoming the elegant residence George Washington wanted it to be when James and Dolley Madison arrived in 1809. The Madisons liked to entertain, and they set about turning the mansion into a suitable setting for their parties.

Dolley focused her attention on three rooms along the south side of the house. Jefferson's former office became—and still is—the State Dining Room. A sitting room next to it was converted into Mrs. Madison's parlor. (It is now the Red Room.) The oval-shaped Elliptical Saloon, the present Blue Room, became the main drawing room.

The splendid rooms provided a superb backdrop for the Madisons' parties, which were the most glittering in Washington. Nothing short of a grave illness could keep people away.

V

James Madison's first term marked the high point of the President's House thus far. His second term, which coincided with the War of 1812, marked the low point. In the summer of 1814, a British army burned the Capitol, the President's House, and several other government buildings.

Rebuilding the President's House became a matter of national pride. Congress appropriated the necessary funds, and the original architect, James Hoban, was invited to reconstruct his mansion and to finish its still unbuilt north and south porticos as well.

The work was still going on when Madison's successor, James Monroe, arrived in 1817. Monroe ordered the work speeded up and was particularly insistent that the East Room be ready for the large receptions he planned. The workmen had gotten as far as replacing the whitewash on the outside walls with white lead paint (which made the White House an even more popular name), but the north and south porticos were still under construction and the inside was a mess.

Nevertheless, the Monroes moved in and Elizabeth Monroe set about decorating the house with furniture they had ordered from France. If the workmen's materials were removed, the President's House would at least be fit to entertain in. James Monroe gave the order, the materials were stashed away, and on New Year's Day, 1818, the president and first lady invited the public to a gala reception. When it was over, the materials were replaced and work on the house resumed.

The Monroes continued this practice whenever they entertained, but the work stopped when the country was hit by the Panic of 1819 and did not resume until the economy improved. The building was finally completed in 1830, not long after Andrew Jackson moved in, and thirty-eight years after it was started.

VI

For almost a hundred years, the president's office competed for space on the second floor with the chief executive's family.

This meant that visitors to the mansion were constantly trekking up and down stairs, allowing first families little privacy. As the responsibilities of the president increased, particularly during the Civil War, more work space was needed, impinging still further on the first families' living arrangements.

With President Benjamin Harrison's arrival, however, additional space became crucial. The Harrison household included their daughter, her husband, and their two-year-old son and baby daughter; Mrs. Harrison's ninety-year-old father; and a widowed niece. With so many people in residence, there was little room and even less privacy. Caroline Harrison tried to free up space by using the state rooms as family sitting rooms, but it soon became apparent that the only solution was expanding the building itself.

Mrs. Harrison consulted an architect, who drew up a plan that would add wings at either end of the mansion. The one on the west would provide office space for the president, leaving the entire second floor available for his family.

The plan got a warm welcome in the Senate but it came to a dead stop in the House. The Speaker, brooding about the fact that President Harrison had failed to appoint one of his friends to a federal job, refused to bring it to the floor.

VII

In 1900, as part of the program celebrating the centennial of Washington, D.C., a symposium was held to discuss the need for improving the city's appearance. In the years since Pierre L'Enfant laid out his plan for the Federal City, public buildings had been put up in a variety of architectural styles. Vacant land was overgrown with ratty-looking patches of grass and fouled by grazing livestock. Railroads ran up and down the streets and crisscrossed the Mall, and there were a half-dozen different terminals scattered around the city.

Prompted by the symposium, Senator James McMillan, a member of the Committee on the District of Columbia, appointed a commission to develop and improve the city's parks. Its members, who were among the leading tastemakers of the day, quickly recognized that a lack of parks was only the beginning of the city's problems.

The commission drew up the McMillan Plan, based on Pierre L'Enfant's original design for Washington, which called for a city of stately buildings, beautiful vistas, and manicured lawns and parks. L'Enfant, who had been booted out in disgrace a little more than a hundred years earlier, would have been delighted to learn that he had suddenly become a hero and that his vision of the nation's capital would finally be realized.

Essentially, the McMillan Plan created the Washington of today, with federal buildings clustered around the Capitol, and Union Station replacing the street-level railroad tracks and individual terminals. The Arlington Memorial Bridge was designed to line up with the Custis-Lee Mansion across the Potomac, and the yet-to-be-built Lincoln Memorial would be situated in a direct line with the Washington Monument and the Capitol.

The White House, possibly the most prominent building in Washington, was high on the McMillan Commission's list of items that needed attention. One suggestion, resurrecting the plans drawn up by Caroline Harrison's architect, had already been vetoed. The projected east and west wings were almost as large as the White House itself. Worse yet, they were capped by glass domes, adapted from the French style that was popular at the time.

Another suggestion, also tabled, was to convert the White House into an executive office building and build a new presidential home on the grounds of the U.S. Naval Observatory, where the official residence of the vice president now stands.

VIII

The McMillan Commission's activities were suspended after President William McKinley's assassination in 1901. His successor, Theodore Roosevelt, had no immediate interest in revamping his new home except to issue an order changing its official name from the Executive Mansion to the White House.

The president's indifference to his living quarters was short-lived. With six children and an assortment of pets, the Roosevelts were squeezed into a home that had too few bedrooms, bathrooms, and closets. The kitchen was old-fashioned and grimy, the State Dining Room was too small, and the floor had to be propped up with ten-by-ten-inch timbers whenever there was a large party in the East Room.

The president asked Congress to appropriate $16,000 for repairs and redecorating and Edith Roosevelt sought the advice of Charles McKim, a member of the McMillan Commission and a partner in the renowned New York architectural firm of McKim, Mead and White.

After a careful inspection of the building, McKim reported

that the $16,000 appropriation would not even come close to covering the cost of everything that needed to be done. With the support of Senator McMillan, McKim persuaded Congress to vote a staggering $475,000 to remodel the White House and build a separate executive office building for the president and his staff.

Charles McKim's 1902 renovation produced the look that characterizes the present-day White House. The remains of Thomas Jefferson's east and west wings were rebuilt, and a complex of greenhouses on the west side of the White House was replaced by a "temporary" Executive Office Building—today's West Wing.

McKim's work on the inside of the house was even more extensive. He transformed the gloomy utility areas in the basement into a series of rooms that could be used for social functions and converted the attic into servants' quarters and workrooms.

McKim took a dim view of most of the furnishings purchased during previous administrations and had them carted off to be sold at auction. If the architect had had his way, the Victorian furniture that is now in the Lincoln Bedroom would have been hauled away as well. But Edith Roosevelt liked it and her husband respected its historical significance. Thus, the old-fashioned rosewood bed was saved, along with a dresser, wardrobe, and circular table.

Theodore Roosevelt, with his strong sense of history, continued to work in the White House, as presidents had been doing since John Adams's day, and used McKim's temporary Executive Office Building as headquarters for his staff.

William Howard Taft would have preferred to continue this tradition, but he recognized the value of having the entire executive branch in a single location. Shortly after he took office in 1909, Taft hired an architect to enlarge McKim's Executive Office Building. A key part of the plans was an Oval Office for the president, its shape chosen in homage to James Hoban's design for the Blue Room.

During Franklin D. Roosevelt's administration, the Oval Office was moved from the center of the West Wing, as the Executive Office Building was now being called, to the southeast corner where it looked out on the Rose Garden that had been planted by Woodrow Wilson's first wife, Ellen, in 1913.

IX

In 1945, soon after we moved into the Big White Jail, as Dad called it in his wryer moments, he asked the commissioner of public buildings to give the place a thorough going-over. He knew that any building as old as the White House needed to be inspected at regular intervals to make sure it was structurally sound.

A year went by and nothing happened, until the evening of an official reception in the East Room. Mother and Dad made their entrance down the Grand Staircase from the second floor, preceded, as usual, by a color guard of four servicemen carrying the American and the presidential flags. As the color guard came marching across the room, Dad looked up and saw the huge chandelier above his head swaying. He lost no time in reporting it to the commissioner of public buildings, but it was several weeks before anyone got back to him. When they did, they didn't exactly pick the best time.

Dad was hosting the last official reception of the 1946–47 season and the guests were being treated to a concert by pianist Eugene List. Howell Crim, the chief usher, and Jim Rowley, the Secret Service agent in charge of the White House detail, quietly informed Dad that the inspection team had found that the chain holding up the center chandelier was on the verge of giving way.

Rather than interrupt the concert and ask his guests to leave—after all, the chandelier weighs twelve hundred pounds—Dad decided that if the chain hadn't broken yet, it would probably hold up for a little while longer. Nevertheless, his first order of business the next day was to have the chandelier taken down. Not long after that, one of the White House butlers came into Dad's study with his breakfast tray and the floor began to sway. This time, the commissioner of public buildings was *ordered* to bring in a team of engineers to check things out.

X

Meanwhile, Dad had set off a few vibrations of his own. In the summer of 1947, he decided to add a second-floor balcony to the South Portico. I won't deny that Dad was thinking of the comfort of the first family. An upstairs balcony would provide us with a pleasant outdoor sitting room. But Dad's interest in the balcony had a strong practical side. In warm weather, the South Portico was protected from the sun by awnings hanging between the columns. The effect was not particularly attractive, especially when the awnings got covered with mildew during the humid Washington summers. The balcony would eliminate the need for these cumbersome, unsightly things.

Dad presented his idea to the Commission of Fine Arts, which had to be consulted about any changes to the White House. The commissioners voted unanimously to reject it. Since the commission did not have the power to block Dad's plan and Congress had already voted a general appropriation that would cover the cost, Dad went ahead with the balcony. You should have heard the uproar! He was condemned for meddling with a historic monument, accused of being an ignoramus about architecture, and called an assortment of names that are not worth repeating.

As usual, Dad ignored the fuss. The Truman balcony was built and the baggy awnings were replaced by a set of good-looking blinds that rolled up and down like window shades. Before long, the Truman balcony began to look as if it had always been there. Several experts on historical architecture have praised its design, and more than one presidential family has told me how much they enjoyed it.

XI

The balcony quickly became old news as a new problem loomed on the horizon. The engineers who had been ordered to "check things out" when Dad felt the floor swaying had come back with a gloomy report. The second floor, where we lived, was about to fall and the ceiling in the State Dining Room would come crashing down with it.

Spurred on by the threat of a cave-in, Dad appointed another committee of engineers and architects to inspect the entire White House. Their report was not reassuring. The foundation was sinking into the swampy ground and the ceiling in the Green Room was held up by only a few rusty nails. If any further evidence was needed that the White House was falling apart, it came in the summer of 1948 when the piano in my sitting room broke through the floor. One of its legs wound up jutting into the family dining room below.

That did it. Dad was banished from his bedroom and forbidden to use his bathroom lest it collapse and land in the Red Room. Mother and I spent most of that summer in our home in Independence, Missouri, and in the fall we joined Dad on the whistle-stop tour that led to his upset victory in the 1948 presidential election.

By the time we returned to the White House in November, the engineers and architects had concluded that it would be dangerous for us to live there. The first and second floors were supported (so to speak) by the same wooden beams that James Hoban had installed when the White House was rebuilt after the War of 1812.

Not only were they rotting with age, they were riddled with gashes made by several generations of workmen sawing into the wood to install new plumbing and wiring. After further inspection the experts determined that the entire house would have to be gutted and rebuilt from the ground up. The only thing that could be saved was the outside walls.

The Trumans moved across the street to Blair House, the lovely 1824 mansion that is the president's official guest house, and construction crews took over 1600 Pennsylvania Avenue. By the time they were finished in 1952, a new White House had risen out of the shell of the old one. Dad was always proud of the fact that his administration had overseen the construction of a White House that would last for ages to come. Mother and I agreed with him. But we would have been happier if another first family had gotten stuck with the disruptions.

XII

Furnishing the rebuilt White House was the responsibility of the building commission, but their decorating couldn't compare to the later efforts of Jacqueline Kennedy, who set out to make the White House not just a well-furnished mansion but a repository of American history.

To ensure that Jacqueline Kennedy's valuable acquisitions would not be jettisoned in some future redecorating project, Congress passed a special act making all the items belonging to the White House part of a permanent collection and preserving the museum character of the State Rooms in perpetuity.

Although it is not generally known, President Richard M. Nixon sponsored an even more ambitious acquisition of antiques. His wife, Pat, had the State Rooms redesigned in the style of the period they represented. Together, the Nixons created the beautiful and historically accurate rooms that exist today.

XIII

Every time I visit the White House, I am reminded of all the people at every level who have contributed to its grandeur. If I had to name names, I would single out for their extraordinary contributions George Washington, who had the foresight to realize how important the nation and its president would become; James Hoban, who created such an enduringly elegant design; and Harry S Truman, who made sure the White House will still be standing long after the rest of us are gone.

Questions for Discussion

1. Do you think George Washington was right in insisting that the nation's leader should live in an impressive house?

2. What are the most important changes that have been made to the White House in the course of its history?

3. Why is it a good idea to have the State Rooms decorated with historically accurate furnishings that are part of a permanent collection?

☆   ☆   ☆

We have Lady Bird Johnson to thank for the handprints of presidential grandchildren set in the paths of the Children's Garden. Credit: White House Historical Association

3

The President's Park

I SELDOM VISIT the White House without pausing to contemplate a venerable tree that graces the south front. Known as the Jackson magnolia after the president who planted it, those gnarled old limbs provided shade on the muggy August day when Harry S Truman had lunch with Franklin D. Roosevelt not long after Dad had been nominated to run with FDR in 1944.

It did not take my father long to realize the rumors about Mr. Roosevelt's declining health were all too true. The president's hand shook so violently, he could not spoon sugar into his coffee. FDR asked Dad how he was going to campaign. When Dad said he was thinking of using a plane, the president shook his head. "One of us has to stay alive," he said. That was the day Harry S Truman realized he might become president of the United States.

That meeting is a good example of why no story of the White House can be complete without an exploration of the acres of grass and gardens and trees that surround it. The history of the grounds is as full of unexpected twists and turns as the history of the mansion itself.

The first president to take a serious interest in the White House's potential for natural beauty was Thomas Jefferson. He planned a landscaped park with small groves of trees and clumps of rhododendron and other shrubs. He marked off one area as the "garden" where vegetables and flowers would grow, fenced off about eight acres of the land set aside for a "President's Park," and made plans to build a high stone wall at the south end of the property.

Although he never got around to doing much about his plan, Jefferson planted scores of seedling trees. Sadly, most of his plantings were trampled by British troops and the army of workmen who arrived to rebuild the mansion after the British burned it.

II

The next president to exert an influence on the grounds was John Quincy Adams, who had a lifelong interest in horticulture. Soon after John Quincy took office, he fired Charles Bizet, whom James Monroe had hired as "Gardener to the President of the U. States," and replaced him with John Ousley, who became almost as permanent a part of the mansion's landscape as the trees and flowers he planted.

Under President Adams's guidance, Ousley devised a park that included seedlings gathered from all parts of the country. Soon walnut, persimmon, willow, oak, and other trees were growing on the White House grounds and a two-acre garden had been planted near the south entrance gate.

The president took an intense interest in Ousley's work and often arose at dawn to do some digging of his own. One morning he wrote of planting "eighteen whole red-cherries." By the summer of 1827, a delighted Adams was bragging to his diary that the two acres contained over a thousand different trees, shrubs, hedges, flowers, and vegetables.

III

John Quincy's successor, Andrew Jackson, had more ambitious plans for the White House grounds. Jackson called in the public gardener of the city of Washington, Jemmy Maher, to help him overhaul the President's Park.

At some point in the course of this work, the White House's most famous tree, the Jackson magnolia, was supposedly planted. There is no written record of its arrival, and some experts have expressed doubts about the tree's origin. One thing we know for certain is that Jemmy Maher and his workmen planted dozens of trees. Among his best selections were horse chestnuts, which produced beautiful white blossoms that added an exotic dimension to the White House grounds.

Another clever purchase, warmly approved by Jackson, was a miniature fire engine, which could be trundled around the grounds, spraying water on the grass and plants along its way. Between the "watering machine" and a hand-pushed roller, the White House lawn became a perfect shade of green and so smooth it looked sculpted.

In 1835, President Jackson supervised the installation of an orangery—a hothouse where plants could be cultivated year-round so that residents of the White House could enjoy fruit and flowers during the winter months.

Jackson's orangery went up just in time to save a Malayan palm tree that had been cultivated from seed in the orangery at Mount Vernon by another enthusiastic horticulturist, George Washington. "Old Hickory," who was an admirer of the first president, took great satisfaction in rescuing the tree after the Mount Vernon orangery burned down. The exotic specimen survived until 1867, when it was destroyed in a second fire, this one in the White House orangery.

IV

John Ousley retained his job as White House gardener through the next four administrations. Among other things, he developed an ingenious scheme for cutting the grass at no cost. When it got knee-high, he let a local livery stable owner cut it and feed it to his horses as hay. Then he called in a farmer, who pastured a herd of sheep there for a few days and reduced the grass by another few inches. By then the lawn was ready for Ousley and his roller to flatten it into a smooth green carpet.

On the east side of the house, Ousley maintained a colorful flower garden. Among his favorite plants were roses, which he trained to climb along a white wooden arbor. Their fragrance undoubtedly contributed not a little to presidential pleasure, especially if you consider the other less lovely odors that swirled in and around the house from the swamps of the Potomac Flats to the south.

Oddly, the presidents and first ladies of Ousley's tenure seldom brought cut flowers into the house. The quacks who passed for doctors in that era had convinced the public that fresh flowers would poison the air indoors. It may surprise you to learn (it did me) that until the 1850s most of the flowers in the White House were wax.

V

The death of President Zachary Taylor in 1850 brought the White House its next amateur horticulturist of note— handsome silver-haired Millard Fillmore. President Fillmore hired Andrew Jackson Downing, the most famous landscape designer of his day, to relandscape Washington's public grounds, including the President's Park, Capitol Hill, and the Mall that stretched between the two.

Downing boarded a Hudson River steamboat at his home town of Newburgh, New York, with drawings of his final plans for the Mall, the Capitol, and the White House. The ship caught fire and Downing died in the flames. His drawings perished with him. In Washington, the president and his aides were too stunned to do anything but lament.

In any case, Millard Fillmore participated in one White House beautification project. He presided at the unveiling of the equestrian statue of Andrew Jackson in Lafayette Square, just across Pennsylvania Avenue from the White House. The square is on land that was originally set aside for the President's Park and it is still considered part of the grounds.

VI

By this time, John Ousley's position as chief gardener was held by John Watt. He persuaded the new president, Franklin Pierce, to let him expand Jackson's rebuilt orangery into a greenhouse. Four years later, Watt's greenhouse had to be demolished to make room for a wing of the Treasury building, but not before plans were made for a replacement. It was to occupy the White House's western terrace and would be connected to the mansion itself to make it easily accessible to presidential families and their guests.

James Buchanan became the first president to use this pleasant patch of indoor greenery when it was completed in 1857. Boasting lemon and orange trees plus dozens of different plants and flowers, the conservatory was furnished with chairs and benches and was gaslit for evening visits.

By this time, fears of being poisoned by having flowers indoors were beginning to wane. The fears all but vanished after Harriet Lane, James Buchanan's niece and official hostess, discovered that vases full of fresh flowers were all the rage in England. She immediately introduced them at the White House, with the conservatory providing a steady supply.

VII

Ulysses S. Grant made two notable additions to the Executive Mansion's grounds. He had a pool installed on the south lawn with a water spray powered by steam, and, in a symbolic gesture signaling a long Republican reign, he had the statue of Thomas Jefferson that President James K. Polk had installed on the north lawn moved to the Statuary Hall at the Capitol. It was replaced by a magnificent circular flower bed with a pool emitting a jet of water at its center.

With the arrival of Rutherford B. Hayes in 1876, the White House had a first couple who were seriously interested in landscaping. One of the president's main concerns was the land to the south of the mansion. In the early days, this was a vast meadow. One section of it was fenced off to create the south lawn, but a large swath of land remained.

Andrew Jackson Downing had hoped to plant trees and grass and turn the area into a large circular "parade" where public celebrations and military reviews could be held. Hayes, drawing on Downing's plan, decided to create a seventeen-acre park called the Ellipse, which became a popular spot for Sunday and holiday outings. Separated from the White House by a curving road, the Ellipse still provides a splendid vista from the South Portico with unobstructed views of the Washington Monument and the Jefferson Memorial.

VIII

The conservatory continued to be popular during the Cleveland and Harrison administrations. It was still a ready source of floral arrangements for every occasion. The orchids that were a favorite during Grover Cleveland's administration were eclipsed by roses during William McKinley's presidency. His wife, Ida, adored them. Her husband was equally fond of red carnations and started a national craze for that flower. He considered them his good-luck charm and never went anywhere without one in his buttonhole.

By 1901, when the Roosevelts moved into the White House, the conservatory had spawned so many annexes that the mansion's west terrace was a veritable village of glass houses, each in a different size, shape, and style. When architect Charles McKim was called in to renovate the White House a year later, the village's days became numbered.

McKim thought they detracted from the White House's formal beauty and would happily have smashed them all into shards, but First Lady Edith Roosevelt was reluctant to see them go. She finally relented, but only on condition that a few of the most attractive greenhouses be moved elsewhere and the most exotic plants be used as the nucleus of a botanical garden for the city of Washington.

IX

Edith Roosevelt called on former White House gardener Henry Pfister to help her design a colonial garden on the west side of the White House where the Rose House had stood. She eventually put in a similar garden on the east side and proudly displayed them both at spring garden parties.

Woodrow Wilson's wife, Ellen Axson Wilson, was another first lady with a passion for plants and a good eye for garden design. Edith Roosevelt's west wing colonial garden was just below Ellen Wilson's bedroom window. As she gazed down on it on Inauguration Day in 1913, an alternative plan entered her mind. She told her daughters it would be "our rose garden with a high hedge around it." A subsequent study of the garden on the east side of the White House marked that one for a face-lift, too.

After consulting with professional landscape designers, Mrs. Wilson decided not only to change Edith Roosevelt's colonial garden into a Rose Garden but to add a tree-lined walkway for the president to use when he went to and from the Oval Office. Prior to that, the nation's chief executive reached his office via the White House basement, trudging past servants' rooms, the laundry, and assorted other utilitarian spaces.

X

When Franklin D. Roosevelt arrived in the White House in 1933, he decided it was time to redo not only the White House but also the grounds. He hired the most distinguished landscape architect of the day, Frederick Law Olmsted, Jr., son of the man who had designed New York's Central Park.

Olmsted approached the task cautiously, with great respect for the old house's traditions. Most of his ideas were gradually introduced, giving the White House grounds the overall appearance they retain to this day. While the property boasts several very colorful gardens, trees have always predominated. One of the oldest of these leafy creatures, an American elm planted by John Quincy Adams, lasted until 1991, when time and disease caught up to it.

Rutherford B. Hayes had hoped to see every president honored with a tree representing his native state. The Ohio-born Hayes started the ball rolling by planting a small forest of

Ohio buckeyes, better known to the rest of us as horse chestnuts.

At last count there were forty-one presidential trees, but
some first families, such as the Bushes and the Clintons, have
more than one to their credit. During their two terms in the
White House, Bill and Hillary Clinton planted a number of
white dogwoods, a willow oak, a littleleaf linden, and an
American elm. Jerry Ford planted an American elm along the
north driveway to celebrate the country's bicentennial in
1976, and George H. W. Bush and Queen Elizabeth II planted
a littleleaf linden to commemorate her visit to the White
House in 1991.

I'm happy to say that Harry Truman has not gone unrepre-
sented. He is responsible for the sturdy and perennially green
English and American boxwood that graces the North Portico. In addition, Dad participated in the preservation of the
celebrated Jackson magnolia. When the White House was re-
constructed under his auspices, Dad watched with approval
while the gardeners dug the old tree from the ground near the
South Portico and replanted it in a safe place. When the restored White House opened for business on March 27, 1952,
the venerable specimen was returned to its original home.

XI

In 1961, John F. Kennedy, perhaps inspired by his wife's determination to overhaul the White House's interior, decided
the Rose Garden needed a new look. The gardening staff had
a few adventures in the course of their digging and planting.
When they replaced the old sod with new dirt, they went

down four inches and found themselves an archaeological treasure trove—pieces of pots from the old greenhouses, Civil War horseshoes, and uniform buttons.

In one corner of the plot, their sharp-edged shovels inadvertently cut the cable for the hot line the president used to put the armed forces on full alert. Within seconds, the gardeners were surrounded by White House police, ready to charge them with sabotaging the nation's security. The cable had originally been laid during World War II, and no one had bothered to note its exact location.

Ellen Wilson's East Wing garden remained pretty much intact until the Kennedy administration. Then JFK, prompted by the transformation of the Rose Garden, decided that its counterpart on the east side of the mansion needed some sprucing up as well. Plans were drawn up but the sad day in Dallas put an end to that dream, along with so many others. Fortunately, Lady Bird Johnson took charge of the garden and saw to its completion. This enchanted spot is often referred to as the First Ladies' Garden but it was officially dedicated by Lady Bird Johnson in honor of Jacqueline Kennedy—a fitting tribute to a first lady whose love for the White House will be remembered for a long time.

XII

The White House also has two very special gardens designed for the exclusive use of the first family and their guests. One is the Children's Garden, created by Lady Bird Johnson in a secluded section of the south lawn. This tiny treasure, which has a small pond in the center, and the names, footprints, and handprints of White House grandchildren set in bronze in the flagstones, was a Christmas present from the Johnsons to the White House.

The second garden, even more secluded than the Children's Garden, is outside the Oval Office, and is for the president's private use. It was created during the Reagan years and remains a closely guarded little preserve—a true secret garden. Presidents occasionally use it on a pleasant day for a lunch or an informal meeting with one of the many VIPs who visit the White House.

XIII

The gardens and grounds of 1600 Pennsylvania Avenue have become so popular, recent chief executives have been persuaded to open them for tours, drawing *oohs* and *aahs* of admiration from thousands. The tours are held in April and October and there is always a long line of people waiting to admire the carefully tended blossoms and critique the first family's taste in flowers. Maybe on garden tour days the president ought to have a sign on his desk that says: THE BUD STOPS HERE.

Questions for Discussion

1. Why were fruits and vegetables planted in the early White House gardens?

2. What are the advantages of having so many trees in the President's Park?

3. What is the most famous White House garden and why is it so well known?

After Richard Nixon's decision to resign as president, he embraced his daughter Julie in one of the most poignant moments in White House history. Credit: Oliver Atkins Collection, Special Collections and Archives, George Mason University Libraries

4

History Happened Here

ON SEPTEMBER 11, 2001, there was serious concern that the White House might become the target of a terrorist attack. Minutes after an American Airlines jet crashed into the Pentagon on that horrifying morning, a squadron of F-16s armed with missiles was airborne over Washington. The pilots had just confirmed the explosion at the Pentagon when the grim voice of a Secret Service agent was heard on their headsets: "I want you to protect the White House at all costs."

As we all know, the White House was spared. If it hadn't been, I hate to think of the toll in human lives and national morale, not to mention the loss of irreplaceable antiques and works of art. It would have been far worse than the previous attack on the President's House that occurred when it was a relatively new and still unfinished building.

In 1812, when America launched a "second War of Independence" against England, no one ever imagined the White House would be in harm's way. It never seemed to occur to the politicians that they were taking on a country that had the most powerful navy in the world.

In the summer of 1814, a British fleet appeared off the Maryland coast carrying an army of 4,500 men. President James Madison called out the militia—part-time soldiers with little training. They met the British professionals at Bladensburg, Maryland, in one of the shortest battles in American history. Although they outnumbered the British, the amateurs ran for their lives at the first volley. President Madison and members of his cabinet, who had ridden out to watch the fight, were swept away in the human maelstrom.

In the White House, First Lady Dolley Madison was trying to go about her normal routine. In the early afternoon, two dust-covered messengers came pounding up to the White House. "Get out!" they cried. "The British are on their way!"

Somehow Dolley procured a wagon, and loaded it with silver and other valuables. She filled trunks with government papers, leaving behind her own and the president's personal possessions. But she refused to retreat, declaring that only a personal command from the president could persuade her to leave.

This command finally arrived in the person of a free man of color who came galloping up the lawn shouting: "Clear out!" The president's friend Charles Carroll also appeared to escort Dolley to safety. As she later recalled it, Carroll was soon "in a very bad humor because I insisted on waiting while a large picture of General Washington was secured and it required to be unscrewed from the wall."

When the White House servants were unable to take down the picture, Dolley ordered the frame broken and the canvas taken out. As she left, she snatched up another precious relic—a framed copy of the Declaration of Independence.

At eight o'clock that evening, the British army arrived in Washington. Without bothering to knock, the men burst into the White House and went to work. They smashed out all the windows and piled the furniture in heaps. Retreating outside, they seized long poles with oil-soaked rags on their ends and surrounded the house. A man with a torch ignited the rags and the poles were hurled through the smashed windows.

Torching the White House proved to be the worst mistake the king's men made in the War of 1812. The United States had been badly divided over "Mr. Madison's War," as they called it in New England. Now the spirit of the nation was aroused. Fort McHenry, defending Baltimore, withstood a nightlong bombardment from the British fleet. In the dawn, a Washingtonian named Francis Scott Key saw the flag still flying and scribbled some verses that became "The Star-Spangled Banner." A few months later General Andrew Jackson scored a decisive victory against the British at New Orleans. Confronted by a united, determined nation, London was more than willing to ratify a treaty of peace.

II

The most famous room in the White House is unquestionably the Lincoln Bedroom—although Abraham Lincoln never slept in it. He used the room as his office. It was here, on January 1, 1863, that Lincoln emancipated the slaves of the eleven seceded southern states.

During the first year of the Civil War, the president had been savagely attacked by the radical members of his own party, the Republicans, for refusing to turn the war into a crusade to free the slaves. Lincoln knew that most Americans were not ready for such a move. At the same time, he detested slavery. From his youth, he had vowed to strike a blow at the awful institution if he ever got the chance.

One day, the president saw a way to do it—by giving the seceded states one last chance to return to the Union. If they refused, emancipation could be called a "war measure," a means to subdue the rebellion.

In the summer of 1862, Lincoln read to his cabinet a draft of a proclamation warning the Confederacy that if they did not make peace by the end of the year, all their slaves would be freed. Secretary of State William Seward urged the president not to release the statement until the Union army had won a victory. Otherwise the move would seem like "the last shriek" of the expiring federal government.

Lincoln agreed and the proclamation was put aside until the Union army repulsed Robert E. Lee's invasion of Maryland in the bloody battle of Antietam. On September 22, 1862, five days after this tremendous clash, Lincoln announced his intention to issue the proclamation.

The Confederacy remained defiant and on January 1, 1863, Lincoln, true to his word, issued the proclamation. Messengers rushed it to the State Department where calligraphers would inscribe it on official parchment. Meanwhile the White House staff prepared for the annual New Year's Day reception. Around eleven A.M., the president and Mrs. Lincoln descended to the Blue Room to greet the diplomats and generals who headed the visitors' line. After shaking hands for an hour, Lincoln felt blisters swelling on his hand and retreated to his office to wait for the proclamation's return from the State Department.

Secretary of State Seward and his son Frederick brought the document over around three P.M. and found Lincoln alone in his office. They spread the proclamation on a table before the fire. Picking up a pen, Lincoln gazed ruefully at his blistered hand. "I never in my life felt more certain I was doing right, than I do in signing this paper," he said. "But . . . my arm is stiff and numb. This signature will be closely examined. If they find my hand trembled, they will say 'he had some complications.' But anyway, it is going to be done."

Lincoln signed in one unhesitating flourish and three million slaves were freed. It was all so low-key, even Lincoln found it hard to believe that he had just executed, as he later told a friend, "the central act of my administration and the great event of the nineteenth century."

III

On April 9, 1865, General Robert E. Lee surrendered at Appomattox Court House. As soon as the news became public, thousands of people poured onto the White House grounds, accompanied by a band. Lincoln came to the north window and startled everyone by asking the band to play "Dixie." He said it was one of his favorite songs.

The next night Lincoln spoke to another crowd. This time he read from a speech outlining his plans to reconstruct the devastated South. Standing among the listeners on the lawn was the actor John Wilkes Booth, who turned to a companion and snarled: "That's the last speech he'll ever make."

Four days later, on Good Friday, Booth committed his terrible crime. The White House was plunged into unparalleled mourning by this first assassination of an American president. Mary Lincoln retreated to an upstairs bedroom and stayed there.

Meanwhile the mansion was draped in black. On Monday night the president's coffin was placed in the East Room and the next day thousands of mourners filed past it. The funeral service was held on Wednesday. Afterward, the coffin was carried in a solemn procession to the Capitol, while a throng of mourners lined Pennsylvania Avenue. A dazed, sobbing Mary Lincoln remained in the White House for another six weeks. The mansion remained draped in its mourning garments until she departed.

IV

In 1803, when the White House was barely three years old, Thomas Jefferson received some astounding news: Napoleon Bonaparte had agreed to sell the vast territory of Louisiana to the United States for about two cents an acre. By a happy coincidence, the news arrived the evening before the president's annual Independence Day reception, when the White House and the President's Park were open to all comers.

At daybreak on that unique July 4, vendors began putting up tents and booths to sell food and drink. At noon the crowds came swarming onto the grounds for what was essentially a country fair. The biggest excitement came not from all this hurly-burly but from the news of the Louisiana Purchase. The sale, which doubled the size of the country, was, without question, the biggest real estate deal in history.

Another historic event occurred on this same Fourth of July. Early that morning, Thomas Jefferson's twenty-seven-year-old secretary, Captain Meriwether Lewis, departed to rendezvous with a Kentucky soldier named William Clark and begin their exploration of the West. The news of the Louisiana Purchase so electrified Lewis that he left his wallet behind in the White House and had to rush back to retrieve it. This gave him a chance to exchange a second farewell with Jefferson, who was experiencing one of those rare presidential moments when everything seemed to be going right.

V

When Franklin D. Roosevelt arrived in the White House on March 4, 1933, the country was in serious trouble. For three years the Great Depression had gripped the American economy. A third of the workforce was unemployed and a staggering 9,106 banks had failed, destroying the life savings of millions.

Two days after his inauguration, FDR closed all the banks in the country to prevent frantic depositors from withdrawing their cash and triggering total economic collapse. On Sunday, March 12, the president announced that he would reopen the banks the next day. He would also give a radio address to the nation that evening to explain the legislation he had pushed through Congress to restore financial stability.

Broadcasting equipment was rushed into the Diplomatic Reception Room, the oval room facing the south grounds that Charles McKim had created out of a former furnace room. At ten P.M., a CBS radio announcer told some sixty million people listening to an estimated twenty million radios: "The president wants to come into your homes and sit at your firesides for a little fireside chat."

That perfect name for FDR's talk was coined by the manager of the CBS Washington bureau. He got the idea from Roosevelt's press secretary, who told him that FDR liked to think of his audience as "a few people around his fireside."

A moment later, FDR began: "I want to talk for a few minutes with the people of the United States about banking. . . ." For fifteen minutes, that marvelous voice coursed across the airwaves, telling the American people that the banking system had been fixed and there was no need to withdraw any more money. In fact, the president went on, it would be safer and smarter to put money into a sound bank rather than keep it under a mattress. "You must not be stampeded by rumors or guesses," FDR said in closing. "Let us unite in banishing fear. . . . Together we cannot fail."

The next day, the newspapers reported in near bewilderment that the banking crisis was over. Instead of runs on banks, people were actually depositing money. Speech experts attributed not a little of this magical transformation to FDR's rich, melodious voice. I also think that knowing the voice was coming from the White House, the symbol of presidential power, had not a little to do with the incredible effect of that dramatic speech.

VI

In 1962 another president found himself dealing with a serious crisis. This White House drama began on October 16 in President John F. Kennedy's second-floor bedroom. At 8:45 A.M., McGeorge Bundy, the special assistant for national security affairs, found the president sitting on the edge of his bed, still in his pajamas and bathrobe.

"Mr. President," Bundy said, "there is now hard photographic evidence that the Russians have nuclear missiles in Cuba."

So began the most harrowing two weeks in the White House's history. Seldom had a president and his administration been so badly surprised. Bundy and others had poohpoohed the possibility that the Soviet Union's alliance with Cuban premier Fidel Castro might lead to nuclear weapons on that controversial island only ninety miles off the coast of Florida. Now they were confronted with enough firepower to destroy every major American city except Seattle.

At 11:45 A.M., cabinet members and advisers poured into the West Wing for the first of many conferences on how to meet this Russian power play. The advisers quickly divided into two camps: those in favor of an immediate air strike to destroy the missile launchers, which could lead to a nuclear war, and those in favor of an embargo on all military shipments to Cuba until the missiles were removed.

As the debate raged, President Kennedy went about the business of the presidency. Occasionally he would slip into the Cabinet Room to see how things were going. Each time, he found the two groups irreconcilable.

On the third day of the crisis, President Kennedy left the White House to attend a luncheon. On the way, he suddenly told his driver to take him to St. Matthew's Cathedral. He hurried into the green-domed church and knelt in one of the pews. Jack Kennedy was not a very religious man. I think the staggering dimensions of the crisis he was facing lay behind this impromptu visit. He had discovered that there are moments when presidents talk to God because no one else can give them the kind of support they need. Lincoln testified to this experience, as did Gerald Ford.

At the end of this harrowing week, John F. Kennedy told his still quarreling advisers what he had decided. The United States would not make a surprise air strike on the Russian missile launchers. Instead, they would blockade Cuba and demand the swift withdrawal of the weapons of mass destruction—or the United States would remove them by force.

This astute combination of toughness and diplomacy proved to be the answer to the crisis. (If it had failed, I would not be writing this book and you would not be reading it.) Faced with a ring of American steel around blockaded Cuba and staggered by condemnations in the United Nations and almost every capital in the world, the Soviet Union backed down and withdrew its missiles.

VII

The Lincoln Sitting Room is a small room next to the Lincoln Bedroom. It had no significant place in the history of the White House until August 6, 1974, when President Richard

M. Nixon stayed there until about two A.M. writing his resignation speech.

The speech marked the end of the Nixon presidency in the
welter of lies and half-truths and snarling vindictiveness of
the Watergate scandal. The trouble began during the 1972
election campaign, when overzealous subordinates burglarized
the offices of the Democratic National Committee in Washington's Watergate apartment complex. For almost two years,
Nixon lied to judges, Congress, and the American people to
defend these men. The situation began to unravel when Congress learned from an aide that Nixon had taped almost every
conversation in the Oval Office.

In late July 1974, on one of these tapes, his lawyers heard
Nixon telling his top aide to use the CIA to restrain the FBI
investigation of the break-in. It was incontrovertible proof
that Nixon had obstructed justice—a doubly serious crime
when it was committed by a president who has taken a solemn
oath to uphold the law. Meanwhile, the Supreme Court had
ruled that the tapes had to be turned over to the special prose-
cutor investigating Watergate.

On July 30, 1974, this most isolated of presidents could not
sleep. At 3:50 A.M. he sat up in bed and began listing the pros
and cons of resigning. As dawn grayed the windows, he decided against it. The following day, however, his top aides listened to the damning tape and came to the conclusion that
resignation was the only option.

Emotional scenes between Nixon and his family con-
sumed much of the next two days. His daughters and their
husbands, along with First Lady Pat Nixon, begged him not
to resign. While the president wavered, his staff continued

to push for resignation. Finally Nixon collapsed once and for all.

When he went to bed that night, the president found a note on his pillow from his daughter Julie. She begged him to delay the resignation for a week or ten days. Nixon later wrote that if anything could have changed his mind, that plea might have done it. But he had already decided to accept Secretary of State Henry Kissinger's argument that his resignation was best for the country.

On August 8, Nixon told a stunned nation: "I shall resign the presidency, effective at noon tomorrow." After breakfast the next morning, the president and first lady said good-bye to the White House staff gathered in the West Hall. A weeping Pat Nixon and daughter Julie followed the president to the East Room, jammed with aides and staffers. The Marine Band burst into "Hail to the Chief" one last time. Nixon gave a rambling speech in which he blurted out an amazingly accurate summation of what had happened to him. "Always remember, others may hate you—but those who hate you don't win unless you hate them, and then you destroy yourself."

After that, the Nixon family went downstairs to the Diplomatic Reception Room, where the new president, Gerald Ford, and his wife, Betty, were waiting. The Fords accompanied them past a military guard of honor to an army helicopter. At the steps of the helicopter, the ex-president shook hands with Ford and ascended the steep ladder. At the top he turned and, to everyone's amazement, managed to summon a smile. The door closed and the helicopter thundered into the blue sky.

VIII

Almost every part of the White House and its grounds are permeated with memories of important moments in American history. I can never look at the North Lawn without remembering August 14, 1945—the day the Japanese surrendered and World War II finally ended. Dad announced the glorious news and then he and my mother went out on the lawn to wave to a huge cheering crowd.

Everyone who has ever lived or worked in the White House has similar associations and memories. We have all had the privilege, and sometimes the pain, of being eyewitnesses to history. In truth, the house itself is history, which is why I and millions of other Americans pray that it will always be protected at all costs.

Questions for Discussion

1. Why did the British burning of the White House turn out to be good for the United States?

2. Of the many historic events that have taken place in the White House which do you consider the most important?

3. What kind of decisions do presidents find most difficult to make?

☆　☆　☆

The State Dining Room in 1873. Back then, dinners lasted four to five hours and had at least six courses. A new wine with each course helped to ease the strain. Credit: Library of Congress

☆ 5 ☆

Working the House

THE WHITE HOUSE is not only a shrine, a symbol, and a piece of living American history, it is also a political tool. In every administration, White House social events—coffees, luncheons, teas, receptions, dinners—have given the president an opportunity to strengthen his relationships with foreign leaders, members of Congress, the party faithful, and just about anyone else who can help him accomplish his programs and goals.

Even crusty, standoffish John Adams saw this potential when he moved into the White House in 1800. Adams held his first formal reception on November 11, 1800, ten days after he arrived in Washington. A week or so later, he and Abigail continued the custom, established in Philadelphia, of inviting Congress to call on them. On January 1, 1801, the Adamses entertained the public at a New Year's Day reception and started a tradition that was to last for over a hundred years.

II

Two days before Christmas in 1963, less than a month after Lyndon and Lady Bird Johnson moved into the White House after the assassination of President John F. Kennedy, and the day the official mourning for President Kennedy ended, Lyndon said to a startled Lady Bird, "Let's have Congress over tonight."

The White House butlers hastily whipped up gallons of punch, and the kitchen staff set to work making enough tea sandwiches to serve to some five hundred congressmen and their spouses, plus presidential staffers and cabinet members—well over a thousand people in all.

It was the biggest short-notice party the White House had ever seen and it was a spectacular success. After the gloom following the Kennedy assassination, everyone was ready for something upbeat. More to the point, LBJ schmoozed with key congressmen and convinced them that he would continue the policies of his predecessor.

III

One of the most amazing things about a White House event is the sheer perfection of it all. Then again, why shouldn't it be perfect?

The White House has a staff of almost a hundred people, including floral designers, chefs, butlers, and social secretaries. There's a chief of protocol to advise on seating; the U.S. Marine Band to supply music; a bevy of military aides, resplendent in their dress uniforms, to keep things moving at the proper pace; and, perhaps the biggest perk of all, a contingent of servants to take care of the cleanup.

When we lived in the White House, I often used to slip downstairs before an important dinner just to take a look at the State Dining Room. It was a truly magnificent sight—the paneled walls, the marble mantel, the dining table set with gold flatware and gleaming crystal and china.

The room is also a mini-museum of American history. Inscribed on the mantel is John Adams's famous prayer invoking blessings on the White House. Hanging above it is George P. A. Healy's portrait of Abraham Lincoln.

There's a small, and fortunately invisible, piece of Truman history in the State Dining Room. Way back in the dark ages—1946—I had a dinner dance at the White House for some of my friends. The party was held in the East Room, but in the course of the evening, one couple wandered down the hall to the State Dining Room.

Intrigued by the massive chandelier that hangs above the mahogany dining table, the young woman asked her escort to lift her up so she could touch it. When he did, she grabbed the metal arms to steady herself. Whereupon he decided to walk away and leave her dangling high above the floor. Fortunately, one of the butlers heard her screams and helped her down.

The young woman and I were the only people who didn't find this prank amusing. Even my father, whom I expected to be as indignant as I was when I told him about it the next day, burst into laughter.

IV

Planning for a White House formal dinner is no easy matter. The guest list, menu, table settings, and floral arrangements are chosen weeks in advance, and the White House kitchen swings into action early in the morning of the appointed day. The menus vary but there are a few rituals that are always the same.

One is the entrance ceremony for the president. It consists of a small parade led by the Presidential Color Team. In my day, they were called the Four Horsemen but now there are five of them, one for each branch of the armed services—Army, Navy, Marines, Air Force, and Coast Guard. Back then, the Air Force was part of the Army.

It is the Color Team's job to go to the president, who is usually in the living quarters upstairs, and request permission to secure the colors. This means removing the American and presidential flags and carrying them down the Grand Staircase to the room in which the president will be receiving his guests. As the president and first lady follow the Color Team downstairs, the Marine Band announces their arrival with a fanfare, "Ruffles and Flourishes," followed by "Hail to the Chief."

At a dinner Jack and Jacqueline Kennedy gave in honor of my father in 1962, my parents and my husband, Clifton Daniel, and I had a private pre-dinner visit with the Kennedys, so we were part of the march down the Grand Staircase. For my parents, it must have seemed like old times, but I had not taken part in the ceremony that often and Clifton was a complete novice. He scolded me for forgetting to tell him that the line of march comes to a halt during the brief pause between "Ruffles and Flourishes" and "Hail to the Chief." As a result, he kept on walking and almost rear-ended Jackie.

By the way, if you've ever wondered where "Hail to the Chief" came from, it's an old Scottish air that was introduced by Sarah Polk for a supremely practical reason. Her husband, James, was not a particularly imposing man and she was afraid he might be overlooked when he entered the room at a large gathering.

V

President William Howard Taft once remarked to his chief military aide, Major Archibald Butt: "The White House is a big political asset when used wisely."

Unfortunately, toward the end of his single term, Taft used the White House unwisely. When he and his wife celebrated their silver wedding anniversary in 1911, they accepted more than a million dollars' worth of silver trays, teapots, and the like, many of them from total strangers who simply wanted to curry favor with the president.

The gifts were a five-star scandal at the time. They'd probably call it Silvergate today. But in spite of my misgivings about that aspect of the event, I have to concede that the Tafts' twenty-fifth anniversary celebration ranks as the most spectacular White House party of all time.

Since their anniversary fell in early June, the Tafts decided to have a garden party. It was to be held on the South Lawn in the evening and the guest list was to include just about everyone they had ever met. The lawn was to be decorated with hundreds of multicolored lights and paper lanterns. The illuminated White House would provide the backdrop.

It took a team of electricians four days to cover all the trees and shrubbery in the President's Park with lights. When they were finished, Taft requested still more lights, including spotlights to showcase the fountain on the South Lawn and the American flag on the White House roof. The flag was to be kept waving by a battery of electric fans concealed behind the chimneys. Some four thousand people attended the party and shook hands with the Tafts beneath an arch with "1886–1911" spelled out in lights.

The U.S. Marine Band, which had been scheduled to stop playing at one A.M., continued until two on orders from the president. Before retiring for the night, Taft gave instructions for the lights to remain in place and the musicians to return the next evening. The South Lawn would be open to the public from eight to eleven P.M. so they, too, could enjoy the spectacle.

VI

If William Howard Taft deserves first prize for the most enchanting party ever given at the White House, Andrew Jackson deserves the booby prize for a pair of wingdings that he hosted. A frontiersman born into humble surroundings and elected by a larger popular vote than any of his predecessors, Jackson was "the People's President" and the people descended on Washington in droves to see him sworn in.

After taking his oath of office at the Capitol on March 4,

1829, the sixty-one-year-old chief executive rode to the White House on horseback. He had about an hour to greet his more important guests before the crowd of some twenty thousand people that had followed him from the Capitol surged past the doorkeepers and swarmed into the President's House.

Many of Jackson's fans climbed on chairs or tables to get a better look at him. Others elbowed and shoved their way to the refreshment tables in the East Room. In the crush, china and crystal were smashed, fistfights broke out, and women screamed and fainted. The president finally escaped through the rear door and headed back to his hotel while the White House steward brewed up a washtub full of whiskey punch and set it on the lawn to lure the revelers outdoors.

You might think Jackson would have learned a lesson from this debacle, but things weren't that much better at his last public reception in 1837. One of his supporters, a dairy farmer from upstate New York, sent him a giant wheel of cheddar cheese. It was four feet across, two feet thick, and weighed fourteen hundred pounds.

Jackson let the cheese age in the White House entrance hall for two years. He finally invited the public to enjoy it at the annual Washington's birthday reception. The city marshal and his deputies were posted at the door to maintain order, but the crowds outwitted them. They poured across the lawn and climbed in the windows of the East Room. Two hours later, the cheese was gone and the mob with it. The floors and rugs were littered with crumbs of cheddar, and the White House reeked of cheese for weeks.

VII

What Andrew Jackson needed, aside from a little common sense, was the small army of military aides who later became a fixture at White House functions. During Theodore Roosevelt's administration, the aides replaced the servants and Secret Service men who had formerly assisted, directed, and, if necessary, evicted guests at official events.

The military aides, who are chosen for their smart appearance, are an attractive addition to White House parties, but their duties go beyond being merely decorative. They are what you might call social traffic cops, charged with seeing that schedules are adhered to, receiving lines keep moving, and ceremonies begin and end on time.

The use of military aides at White House social functions is considered part of their duty to serve their commander in chief. This is also true of the U.S. Marine Band, a group of extremely talented musicians in scarlet uniforms who provide the music for state dinners and receptions and perform on the South Lawn for the arrival ceremonies for foreign leaders.

The Marine Band is the country's oldest professional musical organization. It was established by an act of Congress in 1798 and charged with providing music for the president of the United States and the commandant of the marine corps. Its first White House performance was for President John Adams's New Year's Day reception in 1801. A few months later, the band played for Thomas Jefferson's inaugural, and it has performed at every presidential inauguration since. Jefferson, an accomplished musician himself, affirmed the unique status of the band by naming them "The President's Own."

The members of the Marine Band are graduates of the country's most prestigious music schools. They audition for places just as they would for a major symphony orchestra. Some or all of the band members appear at the White House over three hundred times a year. They may be called upon to provide strolling violinists, a string quartet, or a dance band, and they can probably play "Hail to the Chief" with their eyes closed.

VIII

Entertaining at 1600 Pennsylvania Avenue involves complications and potential pitfalls that are unlikely to bedevil the average host or hostess. Some of the thorniest problems involve visiting royalty. When Princess (now Queen) Elizabeth and her husband, the duke of Edinburgh (now Prince Philip), visited the United States in 1951, my father decided to meet them at the airport. The State Department had a conniption. According to protocol, the president only shows up at the airport to greet heads of state. Dad, being Dad, went anyway.

An early diplomatic crisis arose in 1877 when Rutherford B. Hayes and his wife, Lucy, arrived in the White House. Strong supporters of the temperance movement, they never served wine or liquor in their home in Ohio. They planned to continue this practice in Washington to set an example for the rest of the country.

The State Department feared the ban might provoke an international incident. The White House guest list regularly included diplomats and other representatives of foreign countries.

They were used to having wine with their meals and would be noticeably unhappy if it were omitted.

The first test came early on when two emissaries of the czar of Russia, Grand Duke Constantine and Grand Duke Alexis, visited the United States. Protocol required that they be given a formal dinner at the White House.

The State Department immediately went on red alert. Secretary of State William Evarts regarded it as unthinkable to subject the two young men to a "cold water" meal. To forestall such a possibility, Evarts enlisted the aid of a distinguished attorney who was an old friend of the president's.

In view of what they were accustomed to in their own country, the attorney argued, "a dinner without wine would be an annoyance, if not an affront" to the grand dukes and, by extension, an affront to Russia, a longtime ally of the United States. To Secretary Evarts's enormous relief, Hayes was persuaded.

The dinner was a splendid affair. The State Dining Room was bedecked with flowers, the U.S. Marine Band played a Russian march as the guests filed in to dinner, the food was magnificent, and there were no less than seven glasses at each place, one for water and the rest for each of the six wines that were served. The grand dukes could hardly complain about being annoyed or affronted, although they may have groaned about being hungover the next morning.

IX

In addition to the various dinners that take place at the White House each year, there is also a full schedule of receptions. Some of the receptions start at 5:30 P.M. but the more formal ones usually begin at eight. The guest list numbers about fifteen hundred and everyone has a chance to shake hands with the president. On a number of occasions, I was invited to join Mother and Dad in the receiving line. I didn't mind greeting their guests—most of them were quite pleasant—but I did mind shaking fifteen hundred hands. You can—and I did—incur serious damage to your fingers from pressing that much flesh.

"Handshakitis" is a common complaint among White House residents. Is there anything that can be done to avoid it? I've made a little study of the issue, with some help from several presidents. Early in his career Harry Truman examined the problem with the thoroughness that he brought to all aspects of any job he tackled. Dad decided that the essence of survival handshaking was timing. You should seize the other person's hand before he or she grabbed yours. You should always slide your thumb between the other person's thumb and index finger, so that you, not he or she, did the squeezing.

Some presidents and first ladies have devised alternatives to the handshake. Edith Roosevelt held a bouquet of flowers in both hands, exempting her from the need to endure mashing. Instead of letting his own hand get crushed, Bill Clinton often used both hands to deliver a friendly democratic squeeze—without getting squeezed in return.

X

It may be hard to believe, but the president used to hold receptions on New Year's Day and the Fourth of July to which everyone in Washington was invited. I should hasten to add that they didn't all come. The social elite were almost always on hand but the working classes, realizing that neither their clothes nor their manners were suitable, mostly stayed home.

In James Monroe's era, New Year's Day receptions attracted about a thousand people, but as Washington grew into a full-fledged city, the crowds grew progressively larger. By Grover Cleveland's day, the number had risen to six thousand, putting an inordinate amount of stress on both the president and the White House floors. Calvin Coolidge, already on his way out of office, dispensed with the 1929 event and spent the holidays in Florida instead. I can readily identify with his excuse: He and his wife were sick of getting bruises from shaking so many hands.

Herbert Hoover revived the tradition and between noon and 3:30 P.M. on New Year's Day, 1930, he shook hands with an incredible 6,348 people. Hoover repeated his performance in 1931 and 1932, but that was the last New Year's Day reception at the White House. In 1933 the lame duck president followed Coolidge's example and decamped to Florida for the holidays. Between the Great Depression, World War II, and the burgeoning population of Washington, the receptions were never revived.

Still, you can't say they didn't have a good run. One hundred and thirty-one years is pretty impressive. The Fourth of July receptions, on the other hand, never even came close. They were started by Thomas Jefferson in 1803 and ended by Martin Van Buren in 1839.

Van Buren hated the crowds that poured into the White House for his New Year's Day and Fourth of July receptions, and his guests usually came away hating him. To keep them from staying any longer than was absolutely necessary, he refused to serve refreshments, which were the main reason most of them came.

Van Buren was particularly impatient with the Fourth of July receptions, which interfered with his summer escape to New York. Determined to find a way out, he let it be known that the president would be out of town on July 4, 1839, and the White House would not be open for callers. Presumably his successors were equally eager to escape Washington's beastly summers. Never again was there a reception on the Fourth of July.

XI

About fifty thousand people attend White House dinners and receptions each year. I am convinced that the White House catering staff deserves most of the credit for their success. Usually, they have a little more lead time than Lyndon Johnson gave them in 1963. But they are used to working miracles on short notice.

When former prime minister Ehud Barak of Israel visited the White House in 1999, Bill and Hillary Clinton planned an official working visit that included a luncheon for eighteen people. When word of Barak's arrival got out, so many people wanted to meet him that on five days' notice the luncheon for eighteen turned into a dinner for five hundred.

Eleanor Roosevelt, who could never be called a social butterfly, was nevertheless a demon hostess. She was forever inviting supporters of the many causes she espoused to the White House for tea. There were so many of these gatherings that she frequently had two a day. One of my favorite White House staff members, Alonzo Fields, used to call them "double-header teas."

Lou Henry Hoover gave Eleanor Roosevelt a run for her money when it came to inviting people to the White House. In 1932 alone, she presided at forty teas and held receptions for eighty different organizations. She and the president were also quick to extend luncheon and dinner invitations, often on very short notice. Once, after ordering food for a one o'clock luncheon for six people, Ava Long, the White House housekeeper, was informed a half hour before the guests were due to sit down that the number had changed to forty.

Mrs. Long instructed the cook to grind up every morsel of food she could find in the refrigerator and mix up a batch of croquettes. The end product was served with a mushroom sauce and several guests actually raved about it. When one woman asked what the dish was called, Mrs. Long replied tartly, "White House Surprise Supreme." The housekeeper pulled off another surprise supreme when she handed in her resignation not long afterward.

XII

My favorite example of staff inventiveness was told by my friend Fields (the White House maître d'hôtel and butlers are always called by their last names) some years after he left the White House.

When the Twenty-first Amendment repealing Prohibition was ratified in 1933, President Franklin D. Roosevelt was deluged with gifts from wineries all over the world. Little of it was good enough to serve at the table, but FDR was too much of a penny-pincher to throw it away, so Fields was instructed to find a way to use it up.

Punch is one of the standard drinks at White House receptions. For a crowd of 1,200 people, Fields and his staff would prepare about 45 gallons of fruit punch for the nondrinkers and 110 gallons of spiked punch for those who liked stronger stuff, obviously the majority. Fields uncorked a few of the gift wines and went to work experimenting with various combinations until he came up with several recipes that passed his taste test. One of the most lethal contained muscatel, sauterne, applejack, and scuppernong. Another, only slightly less dangerous, combined blackberry wine, claret, sake, and sherry.

It didn't take long for the wines to disappear, but Fields occasionally had twinges of anxiety. "I could always see the headline," he said. "President's party has tragic end. Guests go berserk after drinking spiked punch at the White House. Chief Butler being held for investigation."

Questions for Discussion

1. What purposes do White House social events serve?

2. Why do White House dinners have to be carefully planned?

3. What is the value of having an entrance ceremony for the president?

☆　☆　☆

Dolley Madison personified the wise use of womanpower. Her warmth and wit won several political battles for her brilliant but reserved husband. Credit: White House Historical Association (The White House Collection)

☆ 6 ☆

Womanpower

I FIND IT amusing that the East Wing, which was built by Charles McKim in 1902 to provide a visitors' entrance and coatrooms, and rebuilt by Franklin D. Roosevelt to add extra office space during World War II, stands on the site of Thomas Jefferson's henhouse. I wonder what Jefferson would say if he could see the flock of females who are hanging out there now—the first lady's staff and sometimes the first lady herself, plus the predominately female White House social office.

There is irony at work here. Thomas Jefferson did everything in his power to keep women, except for scullery maids and laundresses, out of the President's House. Convinced that women should have nothing to do with politics, he hoped to inspire a tradition whereby all the social events in the White House were relentlessly male.

In the Washington, D.C., of his era, Jefferson's attitude all but paralyzed the government of the United States. Politics is not an art form that can be confined to legislative halls. It includes a vast amount of personal give-and-take at social events where women can smooth the rough edges of quarrelsome males.

Aside from all this, the president's deliberate exclusion of women infuriated them. They found their opportunity for revenge after President Jefferson gave a dinner for the new British minister, Anthony Merry, and his wife, Elizabeth. Ignoring the rules of etiquette, he let his guests find their own places at the table. When Mrs. Merry's husband, the guest of honor, was seated far from the president, she persuaded the minister not to accept any further invitations to the White House.

Jefferson denounced Mrs. Merry and blamed her for the problem. But he soon discovered that the women of Washington took Elizabeth Merry's side. Without quite saying so, they admired her refusal to let the "Democratic Emperor," as some of Jefferson's enemies called him, push her around. Prominent among the secret sympathizers was none other than Dolley Madison, the wife of the secretary of state.

Jefferson worked himself into a near frenzy defending his behavior. But the ladies of Washington flocked to Mrs. Merry's dinners, and the president slowly realized he had lost his battle to keep women out of politics.

II

If Jefferson had any doubts about his defeat, they vanished when James Madison was elected in 1808 and Dolley became the first lady. Already well known as a hostess, she swiftly made it clear that ignoring the rules of etiquette and men-only dinners in the White House were as dead as the dinosaur bones ex-president Jefferson liked to collect.

For openers, Dolley staged the first inaugural ball at nearby Long's Hotel. Attended by over four hundred people, it was heralded as "a handsome display of female fashion and beauty." Next, Dolley turned the White House into a political and social power center, with the two ideas so intertwined that no one could tell the difference.

Womanpower. The term did not exist in the nineteenth century, but the White House came to personify it. The State Dining Room became the scene of weekly formal dinners for as many as thirty men and women, with Dolley at the head of the table, presiding over the conversation. At Dolley's Wednesday evening receptions in the Elliptical Saloon, today's Blue Room, she engaged in conversation that was often highly political but simultaneously amusing and informative.

Few doubt that Dolley was responsible for her husband winning a second term in 1812. The warm atmosphere at her parties and her ability to make each guest feel important worked wonders on the congressmen and senators who could have blocked his nomination. By that time, if Dolley were mean-spirited (she wasn't), she might well have asked: "By the way, whatever became of that guy with the silly ideas about women—Tom Jefferson?"

III

Dolley Madison singlehandedly transformed the White House into a public platform for womanpower. The next first lady to take advantage of this breakthrough was Louisa Catherine Adams, the wife of John Quincy Adams. Beautiful, charming, a gifted musician and writer, Louisa had only one problem: her husband. John Quincy had political ambitions, intense ones, but no political abilities whatsoever.

When Adams became secretary of state under James Monroe, Louisa decided she was his only hope of winning the White House. She plunged boldly into the swirling social stream and emerged as her husband's campaign manager, or perhaps a better term would be party chairman.

Louisa began giving a weekly dinner party and launched "Mrs. Adams's Tuesday nights" in which men and women mingled in a convivial atmosphere reminiscent of Dolley Madison's drawing rooms. In 1822, Louisa topped everyone, including herself, with a New Year's Eve party for five hundred.

Thanks to Louisa, John Quincy Adams won the presidency in 1824. I wish I could say the result was four years of triumphant happiness. Alas, the opposite was the case. John Quincy proved to be a poor president. A lot of his problems arose from the close election, which was decided in the House of Representatives. Louisa's partying paid dividends there, but Andrew Jackson, who won the popular vote, accused Adams of making a "corrupt bargain" with another contender, Kentuckian Henry Clay, to win his votes by making him secretary of state. The accusation wrecked Adams's relations with Congress.

Still, no one could take away Louisa's triumph; to this day she remains the only female campaign manager to put her candidate in the White House.

IV

The White House has empowered women other than presidents' wives. Among the least recognized members of this group are the women who operated as substitute or stand-in first ladies for bachelor or widowed presidents or for those whose wives were ill or simply not interested in serving as White House hostesses.

The first of these stand-in first ladies was Andrew Jackson's niece, Emily Donelson, who was married to her cousin, the president's private secretary, Andrew Jackson Donelson. Although Emily was only twenty-one when she came to Washington, she had been born on a Tennessee plantation, and was unintimidated by either the size of the White House or its social responsibilities.

Despite her busy family life—three of her four children were born at the White House—Emily did a good job as hostess and household manager. In addition to being a model of tact, she was one of the few people who was not afraid to stand up to the notoriously fierce-tempered Jackson.

The next president, Martin Van Buren, was also a widower. He spent his first two years in the White House without a hostess. Then his son Abraham married a twenty-two-year-old South Carolina belle named Angelica Singleton, who soon took over the social side of the White House.

Angelica was a niece of Dolley Madison's—it was Dolley, in fact, who had masterminded her match with Abraham Van Buren—but in at least one respect Angelica lacked her aunt's political savvy. During her honeymoon in Europe, she picked up a somewhat dubious custom. Instead of standing in a receiving line, getting her pretty hand mashed, she posed on a platform at the south end of the Elliptical Saloon with flowers in her arms and hair. She wore a gorgeous white dress and surrounded herself with a half dozen women friends, also in glowing white.

The youthful Queen Victoria was posing thus in London. But this was democratic America and Angelica's posing was greeted with cries of political outrage, mingled with sarcastic yawps. Angelica finally got the message and started shaking hands.

V

The proxy first lady who may have enjoyed the job most was Harriet Lane, the vivacious niece of bachelor president James Buchanan. Ignoring the storm clouds of the oncoming Civil War, twenty-seven-year-old Harriet made the Buchanan White House a lively place. Her hair was golden blond, her eyes violet, her mouth impish. Young men and not a few older ones swarmed from all directions to attend her parties.

During the Buchanan era, Washington was awash in southern hospitality and Harriet was determined to have the White House lead the way. She kept the place lively right up to the eve of the Civil War. In 1860, the last year of her reign, she presided at the great social event of James Buchanan's administration, the reception of Queen Victoria's handsome nineteen-year-old-son, Albert Edward, Prince of Wales. Harriet planned a series of lavish social events, climaxed by a banquet on a coast guard cutter, appropriately named *Harriet Lane*.

The partygoers steamed down the Potomac to Mount Vernon, where Harriet and the great-grandson of George III paid a visit to George Washington's tomb. Dinner was served on the return voyage with the Marine Band providing music for dancing.

Did the prince have a good time? Four decades later, he personally invited Harriet Lane Johnston to London to attend his coronation as King Edward VII.

VI

The last of the substitute first ladies, Rose Cleveland, proved that good looks were not a prerequisite for the job. Just under forty, Rose was the bachelor president's youngest sister. She was as plain as a fence post and did not try to disguise it. Nor did she make any effort to disguise her intelligence. A teacher in her native Buffalo, as well as a staunch feminist, she believed that women should vote, hold jobs, and have opinions about everything, including politics. As the president's hostess, she did not hesitate to make this clear to his guests.

At first, Washington's reaction was negative. They were not used to women who were more interested in reading and writing than in the latest gossip. But gradually, among a select group, a different Rose emerged. Warm, often humorous, she established lifelong friendships with several members of Washington's elite.

Miss Rose's reign ended when the president married Frances Folsom in 1886 and his sister went back to teaching and writing. Thereafter womanpower in the White House became the exclusive property of first ladies.

VII

The most famous representative of womanpower in the White House seems at first glance in a class by herself. Eleanor Roosevelt towers above the historical landscape these days as a force for tolerance, brotherhood, and human rights. She spoke out for these and other causes in her time, but the stature she achieved after she left the White House interferes with an accurate assessment of her years as first lady. A close look reveals she was not as powerful or influential as we all want to remember her.

Perhaps the clearest proof of the limitations of a first lady's womanpower is the story of Mrs. Roosevelt's brief career as second in command of the Office of Civilian Defense at the beginning of World War II. The head of the agency, Mayor Fiorello La Guardia of New York, was an old friend. But he and the first lady soon fell to quarreling because Mrs. Roosevelt had a bad habit of appealing to the president when she did not get her way.

FDR, who was trying to organize a major war, had no time for minor ones. He put the agency under the supervision of an aide, who said yes to everything Mrs. Roosevelt wanted to do. La Guardia resigned with a farewell blast at the first lady.

Next, Congress began scrutinizing the Office of Civilian Defense. They discovered that Eleanor had put a pair of old friends on the public payroll, neither of whom was doing much work. Someone pointed out that the two were getting the same pay as General Douglas MacArthur, who was ducking Japanese bullets in the Philippines. A firestorm of negative publicity broke out in the media. The friends resigned and a humiliated Eleanor Roosevelt soon followed suit.

VIII

Eleanor Roosevelt's experience illuminates the very tricky problems first ladies face when they try to move beyond the White House to the public arena. Few if any first ladies worked harder than Rosalynn Carter. She toured the country, she whizzed abroad on goodwill missions, she presided at White House receptions, and somehow found time to learn Spanish. *The New York Times* called her "the most influential First Lady since Eleanor Roosevelt." But unlike nonpolitical first ladies, such as Pat Nixon and Mamie Eisenhower, Rosalynn never became the nation's most admired woman in the public opinion polls.

It may have had something to do with the nickname the press fastened on her: "the steel magnolia." It may have had even more to do with the way the voters view the first lady's role: as simply being there. The American people apparently do not like a woman who has not been elected to office to start exercising political power. Running the White House, they seem to think, is more than enough responsibility.

IX

This mind-set became excruciatingly apparent when Hillary Rodham Clinton tackled the very public job of overhauling the nation's health care system. From the start, the venture had problems. Many staffers felt health care might collide with an even more important priority, getting Congress to pass the president's budget. This may have been the reason for a major blunder—the total failure to draw Congress into the loop early in the game.

It took the better part of a year to get the plan in shape for the president to introduce in a speech. Eventually, Hillary testified on its behalf before five congressional committees, and gave bravura performances. From there it was all downhill (no pun intended, I swear!).

Nobody really liked Mrs. Clinton's health plan, not even her husband's cabinet officers, but because she was the president's wife, nobody wanted to criticize it either. Congressmen and senators heaped unctuous public praise on the first lady and deplored the plan behind the scenes. When the 1,342-page bill was finally sent to Congress, there were nine more months of argument that did little but unite the opposition. The bill was never even voted out of committee for consideration by the full Congress. All in all, it was a humiliating experience for both the first lady and her husband. From Maine to California, Hillary's performance had people asking a tough but pertinent question: "Who elected her?"

X

Womanpower in the White House would seem to work best when it is subtle. It is interesting that Dolley Madison had the right idea two hundred years ago, and a modern woman like Hillary Clinton had to learn it the hard way.

From this vantage point, maybe the most influential first ladies are not the ones who do their politicking in public. My favorite example is someone I had the opportunity to watch in action from very close up—Bess Wallace Truman.

Coming into the White House in the wake of Eleanor Roosevelt, my mother made a decision not to even try to imitate Mrs. Roosevelt's model of a first lady. Bess gave only one press conference—to announce she would not be holding any others. She never made a political statement if she could possibly avoid it. But behind the scenes, Bess Truman was as deeply involved in politics as any congressman or senator.

The president of the United States discussed his problems with her with a candor he would never dream of using with anyone else—and she didn't just listen. She gave him her unvarnished advice. Not until I saw Bess Wallace Truman in the perspective of womanpower in the White House did I begin to appreciate her accomplishment. From her point of view, the less people knew about her influence, the better. Her covert political status gave her the freedom of thought and speech she wanted.

A Washington newswoman recently wrote an estimate of Bess Truman and the other first ladies she knew in her fifty years of covering the White House. Bess, she concluded, had "rejected the role of first lady." Citing one of Dad's favorite sayings, "If you can't stand the heat, get out of the kitchen," the reporter maintained that Bess Truman had adopted her own version of the saying, to wit: "If it's too hot for me, I'll get back to the kitchen."

When I read that, I laughed out loud. If there was one room Bess Truman stayed out of, except in moments of dire necessity, it was the kitchen! Somewhere, I suspect, Mother was laughing, too. Without reporters or anyone else catching on, Bess Truman had White House womanpower down cold.

Questions for Discussion

1. Why were Thomas Jefferson's attempts to discourage women's interest in politics doomed to failure?

2. Besides holding office, how can women influence politics?

3. Should first ladies take an active role in public affairs?

☆   ☆   ☆

Harry S Truman and his appointments secretary, Matt Connelly. Matt always knew who should, or should not, be admitted to the Oval Office. Credit: Harry S Truman Library

The West Wing

FROM THE START, people other than presidents and their families have played major roles in helping the chief executive run the country. During the twentieth century, the number of aides, advisers, directors, deputies, secretaries, and assorted other experts—collectively known as the White House staff—multiplied at an incredible rate. They now total some six thousand people working in over a hundred different offices. But the center of the power structure is still the West Wing.

The West Wing contains the Oval Office, the Cabinet Room, a reception room—also known as the Appointments Lobby—and assorted meeting rooms and offices for secretaries and staff members who deal with the president on a day-to-day basis.

Proximity to presidential power gives a certain aura to anyone who works in, or has easy access to, the West Wing. Its denizens have become the subject of TV shows, movies, and novels. Tell-all books have portrayed them as glamorous, devious, and too clever for their own good. Most of these characterizations are pretty far from the mark. The best portrait of a West Wing staffer was drawn by an old pro, reporter Merriman Smith, who offered a no-holds-barred description of what these jobs entail:

WANTED: *Mature man, educated, witty, politically smart, pleasant personality, unlimited loyalty, to serve as senior secretary. Must be willing to work 12–15 hours daily, including nights. No days off or vacations. But travel constantly. Be prepared to take much blame, public criticism, and ridicule. Should have patience capable of listening to thousands of complaints. Ability to say no absolutely necessary.*

"Smitty," as we Trumans called him, was only half kidding. When a new staffer went to work for Herbert Hoover, he asked a senior employee what the office hours were. "From seven A.M. until midnight, except the nights we work late," the bleary-eyed veteran growled.

II

It seems hard to believe now but our early chief executives had no staffs worth mentioning. Most of them made do with a single secretary, often a relative or close friend. Thomas Jefferson's man Friday, Meriwether Lewis, was not related to the president, but their families were old friends and Jefferson had taken an interest in the young man after his father's death.

Lewis lived and worked in a pair of rooms that had been constructed at the south end of the unfurnished East Room.

His job was a snap compared to later presidential secretaries. He had so little to do, he often went hunting in the nearby woods and fields and brought back rabbits and grouse for the White House table. He also took three years off to explore the Louisiana Territory. Jefferson's relationship with Meriwether Lewis was warmer than many other presidents and their secretaries. Long hours and close quarters often made subordinates a target for executive irritability. James Buchanan's nephew, James Buchanan "Buck" Henry, had to put up with barked orders and frequent tongue-lashings. The breaking point came when Buchanan rebuked him for growing a mustache. Buck quit and headed for New York. His replacement was another namesake nephew, James Buchanan II.

III

When Abraham Lincoln was nominated for president by the Republican Party in 1860, he invited a twenty-nine-year-old Illinois newspaperman, John George Nicolay, to be his secretary. Nine months later, with the southern states seceding and civil war looming, they prepared to leave Springfield for Washington, D.C. Foreseeing the immense workload ahead of him, Nicolay suggested engaging a twenty-three-year-old law student, John Hay, as his assistant.

The workload John George Nicolay had foreseen materialized all too soon. The day after the inauguration, he sat down to write a letter to his fiancée back in Illinois. After two sentences, the call bell in Lincoln's office rang. Nicolay did not finish the letter until midnight two days later.

John George Nicolay and John Hay soon acquired the cachet that goes with working in the White House. Outraged public officials and other VIPs sputtered that the two young men were blocking access to the president and not delivering their letters. Nicolay and Hay, in turn, often gazed with less than friendly eyes on cabinet members and congressmen. On one occasion, Hay wryly remarked that rather than pay another visit to short-tempered Secretary of War Edwin Stanton, he would gladly "make a tour of a smallpox hospital."

About Lincoln neither man had any doubts, no matter what anyone else said or thought about him—and he had plenty of critics in those days. Lincoln reciprocated their affection. The two men slept in a bedroom across the hall from their second-floor White House office. On more than one midnight, the chief executive appeared in their doorway in his nightshirt to read them a funny story from a newspaper or discuss a problem he had figured out how to solve when he should have been sleeping. When Lincoln's son Willie died in early 1862, the president stumbled into Nicolay's office about five P.M. and said: "My boy is gone—he is actually gone!" Bursting into tears, he retreated to his own office.

The White House was almost as unhealthy for Nicolay and Hay as it was for poor Willie. Hay compared summer odors from the swamps south of the mansion to "ten thousand dead cats." When one of them was laid low, the other worked twice as hard. Nicolay and Hay's contribution to the eventual victory of the Union was incalculable. Almost as important, they later wrote a ten-volume life of Lincoln that is a starting point for anyone who wants to understand his greatness.

IV

For all their dedication and intelligence, Nicolay and Hay were still very young men. They never achieved the status of presidential advisers. The first aide to rise to this level was Grover Cleveland's secretary, Daniel Lamont.

This shrewd, genial man got to know Cleveland when he was hired to write his inaugural address as governor of New York. Cleveland took him to Washington after his election to the presidency and Lamont was soon the closest of companions. He swiftly became Cleveland's political adviser as well as his man of all work. He was also extremely astute in his handling of the press.

Lamont got reporters on Cleveland's side with a combination of charm and a steady diet of information. One veteran newsman of the era described his approach: "He let the 'boys' do most of the talking and guessing but never allowed them to leave the White House with a wrong impression, or without thinking they had got all there was in the story."

By the time Cleveland returned to Washington for his second administration, he thought so highly of Daniel Lamont he appointed him secretary of war.

V

William Howard Taft was the first chief executive to work in the West Wing, setting up shop in the Oval Office that was built at his request. One of the most frequent visitors to the new office was Major Archie Butt, who had been Teddy Roosevelt's military aide and continued in the job for Taft. Butt adored Roosevelt and his family and at first was underwhelmed by Taft, but he gradually became devoted to him.

Two years before the end of his term as president, Roosevelt had chosen Taft, his secretary of war, as the best man to succeed him. As time went on, Roosevelt began cooling on Taft. Butt tried to bridge the gap between them. When Roosevelt returned from a postpresidential trip to Europe, Taft asked Butt to deliver a confidential letter, inviting Teddy to the White House for a frank talk. Roosevelt declined with a formal letter, in which he addressed Taft as "Dear Mr. President" instead of the usual "Dear Will." The two men finally met while Taft was vacationing in Massachusetts. Butt, who joined them, reported that the conversation was strained and nothing was resolved.

Meanwhile, Archie Butt slowly but steadily shifted his allegiance to Taft. It was a stressful time for the major. As chief military aide, he was in charge of White House receptions and dinners, of which there were many. He was also William Howard Taft's sounding board as the president brooded over his former friend's threat to run him out of his job.

Finally came Teddy's announcement that he would be a candidate for the Republican nomination in 1912—the break Butt had struggled in vain to prevent. The exhausted aide had scheduled a trip to Europe to visit a friend. Now he wondered if he should go.

"I really can't bear to leave him just now," he wrote to an aunt. "I can see he hates to see me go, and I feel like a quitter in going."

The next morning, Butt canceled his reservations. When

he told Taft, the president ordered him to reinstate them. A month's rest would restore Butt to fighting trim, Taft assured him.

So the weary aide sailed to Italy. Together, he and his friend traveled across Europe to England. There they decided to return home on the maiden voyage of the new luxury liner, the S.S. *Titanic*. On the night of April 14, 1912, the two men were last seen on the slanting deck, calmly awaiting the final plunge. They had given their life jackets to women passengers.

President Taft was devastated by the news that Butt was among the dead. "He was like a member of my own family," he said. "I feel as if he had been a younger brother."

VI

Under Woodrow Wilson, the presidential secretary added another responsibility to his chores: congressional liaison. Wilson was fortunate enough to find the ideal man for the job—thirty-three-year-old Joseph Tumulty of Jersey City, New Jersey, a town where politics came close to being the major industry.

Tumulty backed Wilson when he ran for governor of New Jersey in 1910, and gave the college professor a political education second to none. (Wilson later remarked that anyone who does not understand politics after playing the game for a year or two in the Garden State had better go into another line of work.) When Wilson headed for the White House in 1913, he took Tumulty with him. He trusted Tumulty's political judgment completely. He let him decide whom he should see and whom he should duck. He also depended on Tumulty to cajole leaders of Congress into looking with favor on the legislation Wilson sponsored.

Alas, inside the White House, Tumulty found himself confronted by an unexpected enemy: Wilson's second wife, Edith Galt. She was jealous of Tumulty's influence with the president, and persuaded her husband to fire him at the beginning of his second term. A reporter friend of Tumulty's talked Wilson into changing his mind, but their relationship never regained its previous intimacy.

Nevertheless, Tumulty remained devoted to Wilson to the sad end of the president's life in 1924. Few aides have left more emotional tributes to their departed chief. "Yes, Woodrow Wilson is dead," Tumulty wrote. "But his spirit still lives—the spirit that tried to wipe away the tears of the world, the spirit of justice, humanity and holy peace."

VII

Herbert Hoover expanded the White House staff from a secretary and a dozen or so office assistants to some forty people—a number that seems positively minuscule by today's standards. Hoover's staff were anonymous, faceless men operating in the shadow of their boss. In contrast, Franklin D. Roosevelt's staff was twice the size of Hoover's and many of them rapidly became celebrities in their own right.

At the top of the list of Roosevelt aides was Harry Hopkins, a former social worker from Iowa. FDR enjoyed his cynical humor and his ability to get things done. As head of the Works Progress Administration, better known as the WPA, Hopkins spent eleven billion dollars in five whirlwind years and created jobs for 8.5 million men and women.

On the downside, Harry was often too fast with the comeback for his own good. When a reporter informed Hopkins that many congressmen said he was no politician, he sneered: "Tell 'em thanks for the compliment."

Many presidents would have jettisoned such a controversial adviser, but FDR was a stubborn man. He not only kept Hopkins around, he moved him into the White House when his health collapsed in the late 1930s. His illness, a rare form of stomach cancer, did not stop Hopkins from masterminding Roosevelt's bid for a third term in 1940. During World War II, FDR made him an unofficial secretary of state, sending him abroad to talk politics and military strategy with Winston Churchill and Joseph Stalin.

Another staff member who won FDR's trust was his secretary, Marguerite "Missy" LeHand. Missy had been with FDR since 1920, when she worked for him during his failed run for the vice presidency. She lived through his ordeal with polio and followed him to the governor's mansion in Albany. She was thirty-seven when she came to the White House and moved into a pair of rooms on the third floor.

Missy acted far more like a wife than a secretary, boldly disagreeing with FDR in front of others, shopping for him, and making sure he took his cough medicine. "She was one of the very, very few people who was not a yes-man," one aide said.

In 1941, Missy collapsed from a stroke that left her partially paralyzed, and retreated to the home of a sister in Massachusetts. She died in a Boston hospital on July 31, 1944, nine months before the man she called "F.D." died in Warm Springs, Georgia.

VIII

FDR started out with a staff of fewer than one hundred people, but by 1945 the number had increased to 225. Some of the personalities who swirled through and around the Roosevelt Oval Office would make a book unto themselves. The prize for most colorful character undoubtedly went to Major General Edwin "Pa" Watson, a rotund Alabamian who was the Roosevelt White House's court jester. FDR's day invariably started with a visit from Pa, who always had a funny story for him.

Many people thought Watson was just a joker. But he was by no means politically stupid. As appointments secretary, he had a lot to do with who got to see the president. In 1944 he made sure no one who had a good word to say for Vice President Henry Wallace got anywhere near FDR for several months. That bit of infighting played no small part in making Senator Harry S Truman the Democratic nominee for the job. Watson joined this cabal (of which my father was totally unaware) because he knew FDR was dying and the vice president of 1944 was very likely to become president. He and many others thought Wallace would be a disaster.

Watson was an unlikely candidate for the select group of White House insiders who can say they helped change the course of American history. But proximity to the Oval Office almost guarantees such surprises.

IX

The Truman aides who appeared in the West Wing underscored the growing maturity of the White House staff system. Dad was particularly careful about selecting his appointments secretary—no one sees more of the president or needs to be closer to what he is thinking. His choice for the post was Matt Connelly, who had worked for him on the World War II Truman committee.

Matt did more than schedule appointments, of course. He was the "contact man," as he later put it, for politicians across the country when they came to Washington. Not all of them could get to see the president but they all saw Matt.

Matt made a big difference in the 1948 campaign, when Dad, the underdog by umpteen points in every poll, made his famous whistle-stop campaign across the country. Matt's role as presser of political flesh outside the Oval Office put him on a first-name basis with politicians all over the country. One reporter noted that on the Republican candidate's campaign train, "local politicians did not get the red-carpet treatment they received from Truman's aide, Matt Connelly."

The other indispensable Truman aide was Charlie Ross, who literally worked himself to death as press secretary, as I described in the opening chapter. Charlie had enormous prestige with the press corps and was greatly loved by all the Trumans.

X

None of these Truman staff members sought or got the kind of publicity that Roosevelt's aides accumulated. Grandstanding was taboo in the Truman White House. There was only one exception to this rule—a big handsome Missourian named Clark Clifford. Some historians have called him "the Golden Boy" of the Truman White House.

There is no doubt that Clark was a smart lawyer and a polished writer. My father valued his services and his candid advice. But after Clark left the White House to launch a lucrative law practice in Washington, he began taking credit for almost everything the Truman administration did.

A distressing number of reporters and even a few historians believed Clark. They did not seem to realize that the phrase my father had on his desk—"The buck stops here"—was a description not only of presidential responsibility but of presidential leadership. No single White House aide or even all of them put together can claim credit for the big decisions. A president makes them in the lonely hours of his day (or night), after listening to dozens of people.

XI

Succeeding presidents assembled new staffs, who soon displayed some of the tendencies that were already becoming apparent in the post–World War II White House. Infighting and vying for the president's attention were raised to fine arts and an enlarged ego became a predictable side effect of working in the West Wing.

In the all too brief Kennedy regime, another side effect developed. The president emanated such glamour and charisma that his aides could not help sharing the glow. As Dave Powers, JFK's old Boston pal, put it: "He made everybody around him look ten feet tall." After JFK died, Powers added: "Now he's gone and they're shrinking."

The Kennedy staff was relentlessly male. But in their midst was an important woman whom most of them barely noticed: presidential secretary Evelyn Lincoln. In appearance and demeanor, she was neither glamorous nor powerful, but she was capable and, equally important, loyal.

JFK remarked one day to his favorite speechwriter, "If I said, 'Mrs. Lincoln, I have cut off Jackie's head. Would you please send over a box?' She would [reply] 'That's wonderful, Mr. President. I'll send it right away. Did you get your nap?'"

Mrs. Lincoln had far more power than most White House watchers suspected. People could get to see the president through her door when they were turned away by JFK's appointments secretary. But the biggest surprise came when Mrs. Lincoln published her book. While her portrait of JFK is affectionate on the whole, it revealed just how much this birdlike woman saw and remembered. Her JFK did not always wear his famous smile. He often blew his stack and berated everyone in sight, including innocent bystanders. At the same time, the book is a touching story of a country girl from the plains of Nebraska who fulfilled a lifelong hunger for glamour and excitement by getting a job in the White House.

XII

In his memoir of his days in William Jefferson Clinton's administration, Secretary of Labor Robert Reich offers this glimpse of the White House staff.

The Secretary of Transportation phones to ask me how I discover what's going on at the White House. I have no clear answer. . . . The decision-making "loop" depends on physical proximity to B— who's whispering into his ear most regularly, whose office is closest to the Oval, who's sitting or standing next to him when a key issue arises. . . . In this administration you're either in the loop or out of the loop, but more likely you don't know where the loop is, or you don't even know there is a loop.

The Clinton White House may have been more chaotic than most, but in any administration there are always a few aides who are determined to be in the "loop" at all costs. George Stephanopoulos spent four years in the Clinton White House as the president's senior adviser. Young, bright, and photogenic, Stephanopoulos was quickly singled out by the press as one of the stars of the White House staff. Eventually, however, he began to sour on life in the West Wing. Everywhere he looked, including the mirror, he saw vanity, ambition, and a love of power. Add in the long hours, the constant stress, and the ups and downs of presidential moods, and Stephanopoulos decided to preserve his sanity by bailing out at the end of Clinton's first term.

XIII

Some stars, such as Karl Rove and Condoleezza Rice, have emerged in George W. Bush's West Wing, but so far no one seems to have become a golden boy (or girl) or a grandstander. There have been rumors of intrigues and rivalries, backstabbing and betrayals—some of which may actually be true. Such things happen even—or perhaps especially—in the White House. But we will have to wait a few years for insider books to be written and historians to mull over diaries and letters and E-mails before we really know what's been happening. Meanwhile, I continue to believe that, whatever their political views or personal agendas, most of the small army of men and women who work in the West Wing have a genuine commitment to the country. They may never experience the close personal relationship that John George Nicolay and John Hay enjoyed with Abraham Lincoln, but there is a bond of mutual respect and affection. There is also the realization that grueling hours and constant crises are not a bad trade-off for the privilege of serving the president of the United States.

Questions for Discussion

1. What qualities should a president look for in selecting staff members?

2. Why is the job of appointments secretary so important?

3. Why are White House staff members apt to resign after a year or two on the job?

☆　☆　☆

A 1982 photo of the residence staff in the State Dining Room. Do a head count and you'll see why Nancy Reagan called the White House an eight-star hotel.
Credit: Courtesy Ronald Reagan Library

☆ 8 ☆

Frontstairs, Backstairs

SOME OF THE most important people in the White House are all but invisible except to the families who live there. I'm talking about the household staff—the hundred or so men and women who prepare and serve the meals, vacuum the floors, polish the silver, repair the plumbing, check the wiring, and do whatever else is needed to keep the President's House in perfect condition.

Overseeing this large and varied assortment of workers is the chief usher, who is basically the general manager of 1600 Pennsylvania Avenue. He—so far they have all been men—works directly with the president and first lady and conveys their requests to the rest of the staff.

Every change in administration brings a spate of new requests. The day after Lyndon Johnson moved into the White House, he demanded that Chief Usher J. B. West do something about his shower. "If you can't get it fixed," he snapped, "I'm going to have to move back to The Elms"—a reference to the house he and his family had lived in during his vice presidency. West, with a couple of White House plumbers in tow, went up to inspect the offending shower. They found it in good working order, but it was not the superfancy model the president was used to. There was no way to regulate the direction and force of the spray.

Accompanied by the plumbers and the White House engineer, West went out to The Elms to study the shower. It was unlike any they had seen before, but they got in touch with the manufacturer and were able to order a duplicate. The new shower was no sooner installed than the president was on the warpath again. This one wasn't right either. West called the manufacturer again. This time they sent the company engineers to check out The Elms shower and make one that would be exactly the same.

The new shower still didn't satisfy the president so another one was ordered and when that one didn't work, it was replaced by yet another one. The engineer decided the problem was water pressure, so a special tank with its own pump was installed just for the president's shower. But it still wasn't strong enough. West and his staff kept designing and redesigning LBJ's shower, and spending thousands of dollars and untold man-hours in the process, trying to find one that would satisfy him. They ended up with a complicated fixture that had a half dozen different nozzles and sprays, but by the time they finally achieved perfection, Johnson was on the verge of moving out.

When LBJ gave his successor, Richard Nixon, a tour of the White House, he made a point of extolling the wonders of his shower. After one encounter with LBJ's maximum force spray, the new president called the chief usher's office and said,

"Please have the shower heads all changed back to normal pressure."

II

The job title chief usher dates back to Benjamin Harrison's administration. There are various explanations of why it was adopted, but the most plausible one is that in the old days, the top man at the President's House was the man who ushered people in to see the chief executive.

The most durable chief usher in White House history has to be Irwin Hood Hoover, who went by the nickname Ike. Hoover was a twenty-year-old employee of the Edison Company when he was sent to the White House in 1891 to install the first electric lights for Benjamin Harrison. When he was finished, he got a letter from the commissioner of public buildings, offering him a permanent job as the house electrician. Hoover accepted the offer and he soon figured out why it had been made. President Harrison and his family were afraid to touch the light switches for fear of being electrocuted!

Ike would turn on the lights in the downstairs rooms in the evening and turn them off when he came to work the next morning. It took the Harrisons the better part of a year to get up the nerve to use the electric lights in the living quarters. They were equally fearful of pushing the electric call buttons to summon the servants. "There was a family conference every time this had to be done," Hoover wryly recalled.

Ike was promoted to usher in 1904 and became chief usher during the Taft administration, a job he held for the next twenty-five years. In all that time, there was only one problem he was unable to solve. When Herbert Hoover became president in 1929, there were two Mr. Hoovers in the White House. To avoid any confusion, Mrs. Hoover insisted that Ike be referred to as "Mr. Usher."

III

I'm sorry to say that slaves were not uncommon in the pre–Civil War White House. Abigail Adams, the first woman to examine the place with the eyes of a practiced hostess, thought at least thirty servants were needed to run it. She was unquestionably right, but the early presidents tried to cope with far fewer than that number because Congress, already convinced the president was overpaid at $25,000 per year, declined to include the White House in their budgets.

Jefferson tried to economize by importing some of his slaves from Monticello, but he soon decided this was not a good idea. They did not get along with his French steward, who had a poor command of English and an autocratic style. By the end of his first term, Jefferson was telling his daughter back in Monticello that he preferred white servants. "When they misbehave, [they] can be exchanged," he wrote. He meant fired and replaced, of course.

Andrew Jackson imported slaves from his Tennessee estate, The Hermitage. President Zachary Taylor, another slave owner, used blacks from his Louisiana plantation. But a change in the American attitude toward slavery was beginning to take hold in many people's minds. Fearful of political repercussions, Taylor kept his slaves out of sight. They worked only in the second-floor family rooms and slept in the attic. Free blacks, who had previously comprised most of the household staff, were dismissed lest they be mistaken for slaves.

When the Thirteenth Amendment to the Constitution brought an end to slavery in 1865, blacks returned to the White House workforce but they were not always integrated. In President Ulysses S. Grant's administration, the inside servants were white and the outside ones black.

In later administrations, white and black servants worked side by side and those who were entitled to meals ate together as well. This was the norm until 1909, when Helen Taft hired an arrogant housekeeper named Elizabeth Jaffray, who decreed that henceforth white servants and black servants would eat in separate dining rooms.

When Calvin Coolidge discovered the whites were getting better food, he gave orders that the same meals be served to both groups, but it was not until Eleanor Roosevelt got to the White House that anyone addressed head-on the issue of segregation.

Mrs. Roosevelt's solution was to fire the whites on the household staff, except for the housekeeper, and hire only blacks, which solved the problem—up to a point. Integration finally came to the White House during my father's administration. The man who banned segregation in the armed forces in 1948 could hardly tolerate it in his own household. The President's House has been an equal opportunity employer ever since.

IV

It took many years and several presidents to finally convince Congress that the government should bear the expense of running the White House. Until federal funds were forthcoming, only the wealthiest chief executives could afford to hire an adequate staff and host a suitable number of social events.

Congress's decision to allot funds to remodel the White House in 1902 was followed by a willingness to pay for a decent-sized staff. When Woodrow Wilson took office, Abigail Adams's ideal number of thirty had at last been attained. By the time the Trumans got there, Chief Usher Howell Crim presided over a staff of almost fifty people, including two assistant ushers, two electricians, five engineers, five carpenters, seven gardeners, two plumbers, a housekeeper, six cooks, three butlers and a maître d'hôtel, seven doormen, four housemen, five maids, and several typists and messengers. It seemed enormous at the time but now it is twice that size.

V

The transition from one administration to the next is always difficult for the household staff. As of twelve o'clock on Inauguration Day, they have a whole new family to deal with—a new set of personalities, different likes and dislikes, and more often than not, a complete change in routines.

The president's first dinner in the White House is an especially tense occasion. It's hard to be certain what his and his family's food preferences might be, especially on such a busy day. When the Nixons moved into 1600 Pennsylvania Avenue on January 20, 1969, chef Henry Haller and the housekeeper, Mary Kaltman, stood by in the kitchen. They had been stocking up on groceries for the previous two weeks. They knew that steak was a Nixon favorite but, just to be on the safe side, they bought everything they could think of that might please the presidential palate.

That evening, Mrs. Nixon called down to the chef. The president and his daughters, Tricia and Julie, and Julie's husband, David, wanted steak for dinner. Mrs. Nixon would dine in her room and all she wanted was a bowl of cottage cheese.

The steak was a no-brainer but there wasn't an ounce of cottage cheese in the house. Although Chef Haller was sure that every grocery store in the District of Columbia would be closed at that hour, he called for a White House limousine. Minutes later, the head butler was speeding around Washington searching for cottage cheese. Luckily, he found some in a local deli. Mrs. Nixon's dinner was soon served and cottage cheese quickly became a White House staple.

Herbert Hoover and his wife complicated the staff's lives when they insisted that, as far as possible, the servants should keep out of sight. "Heaven help you if you were caught in the hall when the president was coming," one maid recalled.

People dove into closets and empty bedrooms at the first hint that the president or first lady might be on their way. One particular closet on the second floor near the elevator would often be full of butlers, maids, and housemen as the president strode down the hall.

For the residence staff, the arrival of the Franklin D. Roosevelts was like the return of sunshine. When FDR saw people

ducking into closets as he was wheeled toward them in the upstairs hall, he asked what in the world was going on. When
the Hoovers' predilections were explained to him, he told
everyone to relax. There was no reason to be afraid of him or
the first lady.

With every change of administration, the maître d'hôtel,
who is in charge of organizing and serving the food at White
House social events, may be called on to issue new orders to
his staff of butlers. After Richard Nixon's first state dinner, he
complained about the slow pace of the meal and suggested
cutting the soup course. When his chief of staff, H. R. Haldeman, demurred, Nixon growled: "Men don't really like soup!"
Haldeman retreated and called the president's valet, who told
him Nixon had spilled soup all over his vest while trying to
slurp and talk simultaneously. Haldeman fired off an "action
memo" banning soup at future dinners.

The staff has long since learned to be philosophical. They
are there to please the first family. They also know that no
matter how outlandish the tenants' demands become, in four
or, at most, eight years they'll be gone.

VI

White House doormen don't open doors. They welcome
people to the President's House. At formal dinners, they take
the guests' coats and present them with the escort cards that
tell them which table they will sit at.

In the early days of the White House, there was only one
doorman. He lived in a small room or lodge on the west side
of the entrance hall and kept track of who went in and out.

As more and more people started calling on the chief executive, the doorman began keeping a list, which was sent upstairs to the president or his secretary to decide who would be admitted.

If there were a prize for the doorman who witnessed the most history, it would probably go to Thomas Pendel, who became a doorkeeper in Abraham Lincoln's White House and stayed for over forty years. Even in his old age, Pendel retained vivid memories of the night Lincoln was shot. He could bring tears to the eyes of listeners as he told of hugging a distraught Tad Lincoln when the news of his father's death reached the White House.

When Ira Smith, another man who would become a White House fixture, went to work in the McKinley mail room in 1897, he encountered a graying Tommy Pendel.

"I'm the man who let him out," Pendel told him.

"How's that?" young Smith asked.

"The way it was that night," Pendel said. "He come down to the front door where the others was waiting for him. I remember it clear. The carriage was waiting and ready to take them to the theater where some famous lady was performing in a stage show. They was all ready to go and they come over to the door where I was standin' because I was an usher then like I am now. He was walkin' tall and straight and he smiled pleasant-like at me and I opened the door for him to go down to Ford's Theater. I'm the man who let him out."

It dawned on Smith that Pendel was talking about Lincoln on the last night of his life.

VII

The White House doorkeepers had a reputation for being independent but a couple of the housekeepers could give them a run for their money. One of the most difficult was Elizabeth Jaffray, who arrived with the Tafts.

Helen Taft may have been imperious but her housekeeper was a veritable despot. She would not allow her subordinates to sit down in her presence and they could not speak to her unless she spoke first. She also disapproved of automobiles, which were rapidly becoming popular. She dismissed them as "vulgar contrivances" that would never last, without mentioning the fact that she was scared to death to ride in one. When the White House acquired a fleet of cars, Mrs. Jaffray took over President Taft's discarded horse-drawn brougham. It would pull up to the North Portico each morning and the housekeeper would appear wearing a large hat with a veil and toting a parasol, to be driven off to do the marketing.

Elizabeth Jaffray's reign of terror continued through the Wilson and Harding administrations but the tyrant met her match in Calvin Coolidge. Cal started calling her "Queenie" behind her back, refused to treat her with the deference she felt she deserved and, unlike previous presidents, took an interest in what was going on in the kitchen. He revised the menus for state dinners and demanded to know what happened to the leftovers.

After a couple of years of Cal's needling, "Queen" Elizabeth decided to retire. The rest of the staff silently cheered. Coolidge replaced Queenie with a genial dietician from Boston named Ellen Riley. He liked her so much he invited her to join his guests at White House musicales and movie screenings and gave her the combination to the vault where the gold and silver services were stored. He also gave her a wacky title: Custodian of the Plate, Furniture, and Public Property of the Executive Mansion. Despite his public image as a dour New Englander, Coolidge was a master of deadpan humor. Only a few people have noted that at his Amherst College graduation he was chosen by his classmates to deliver the Grove Oration, which gave the college and the professors a farewell horse-laugh.

VIII

Another tyrannical housekeeper, Henrietta Nesbitt, arrived at the White House with Franklin and Eleanor Roosevelt. She had worked as a cook at the Roosevelt home in Hyde Park, and Eleanor, impressed by her frugality, brought her along to Washington. The Roosevelts not only had a large family, they often invited friends for lunch or dinner. Since the president has to pay for his personal entertaining, Eleanor was counting on Mrs. Nesbitt to keep the expenses from getting out of hand.

Franklin D. Roosevelt had always loved good food; quail and pheasant were among his favorites. Fluffy, as the staff referred to the new housekeeper when she was out of earshot, disapproved of such delicacies. "Plain foods, plainly prepared" was her motto. FDR had announced more than once that he disliked broccoli. "Fix it anyhow," Fluffy told the cooks. "He should like it." At one dinner, when the president and his guests requested hot coffee, Fluffy sent them iced tea instead. Her explanation: "It was better for them."

Mrs. Nesbitt also had her own ideas about what the president should eat for breakfast: oatmeal. After one too many bowls of the stuff, FDR exclaimed to his secretary, "My God! Doesn't Mrs. Nesbitt know there are breakfast foods besides oatmeal? It's been served to me morning in and morning out for months and months now and I'm sick and tired of it!"

Later that day, the president ripped out a newspaper ad for several other cereals including Corn Flakes and Cream of Wheat and had the secretary take it to Mrs. Nesbitt as a "gentle reminder."

Unfortunately, the Trumans inherited Mrs. Nesbitt. There was some improvement after Mother took over the meal planning, but when she had to go out of town and left me in charge, Dad and I found ourselves on a steady diet of brussels sprouts. Dad detested the things, but did Mrs. Nesbitt care? Of course not.

I got the impression Mrs. Nesbitt enjoyed ignoring my father's preferences and disregarding the menus I planned. I was ready to evict her on the spot but Mother told me to hold off; she would speak to her when she got back. By that time, Mrs. Nesbitt informed us that she was planning to retire, which saved Mother the trouble of firing her and guaranteed that we would finally get some decent food.

IX

Out of the thousands of people who have worked at 1600 Pennsylvania Avenue over the years, two lemons—Queenie and Fluffy—are not a bad average. In the Trumans' experience and that of other first families I've talked to, the staff gets universally high marks for going out of their way to be helpful.

Barbara Bush was amazed when she arrived in 1989. "By this time I had lived [in] or visited many places but never had seen a household where every living human's only concern was to make us, our children, and our guests happy," she said.

One of my favorite memories of the White House staff underscores Barbara's comment. It involves Alonzo Fields, the tall, personable maître d'hôtel during our seven-year-and-eight-month sojourn. I loved the bread pudding the house chefs prepared to accompany the pheasant they generally served at state dinners. (Now you couldn't pay me to touch anything so fattening.)

At these sumptuous affairs, with everyone in white tie and tails and evening gowns galore, I was seated so far below the salt, I was practically in the kitchen. Seating at these fêtes was (and still is) done by rank, and a president's daughter has none worth mentioning.

With pheasant and bread pudding on the menu, there was high anxiety for yours truly. Were they going to run out before they got to me? The stuff was so popular, it was all too possible. But I soon learned that Fields had stored in his capacious head some precious information about me. One evening, I watched the bread pudding supply dwindle as the butler who was serving it got closer to my place. My hopes sank until I heard Fields call softly into the kitchen: "More bread pudding for Miss Margaret!"

X

The White House staffers have some interesting memories of their own. I particularly like a couple of stories involving my father. Dad was in the habit of doing some work in his private study on the second floor while waiting for lunch to be served. When he left, houseman George Thomas would go in and make sure the room was tidied up.

One day Thomas yielded to temptation and sat down in Dad's big leather chair. Who should appear in the doorway but the chief executive himself, returning to pick up some papers he'd forgotten. "George," Dad said to the paralyzed Thomas, "I'll tell you one thing. You're in a mighty hot seat!"

With that, Dad picked up his papers and returned to the Oval Office and George Thomas breathed an enormous sigh of relief.

Another houseman, Herman Thompson, handled the dozens of phone calls that came into the kitchen from various people both inside and outside the White House. One day Herman answered the phone and a voice he didn't recognize said: "I'd like to order lunch for Mrs. Wallace [my grandmother] and me."

"Who is me?" Herman jauntily asked.

"I happen to be the president of the United States," the voice replied.

The rest of the staff told Herman to clean out his locker. He was definitely out of there. But, of course, he wasn't. Instead of reprimanding him, Dad got a good laugh out of the episode.

XI

Working at the White House has become a way of life, not only for individuals but for families. Johnny Muffler was hired as an electrician in 1945 and celebrated his fiftieth year on the job by making sure every clock in the place was ticking and telling the same time. Johnny's father-in-law had been a chauffeur, and his son Rick worked in the calligraphy office, where the invitations to the state dinners and receptions are penned by a professional staff.

In recent years there have been three butlers named Ficklin: Charles, who later took Fields's job as maître d'hôtel; John; and Samuel. Samuel Ficklin recalled the training he received from his brother, Charles, and Fields before he got the job. He was told to take some bricks and use them to strengthen his hands and arm muscles by hefting them until he could hold a heavy tray without the slightest tremor. He was also trained to set the table with each plate exactly the same distance from the edge.

The tradition of impeccable service and the determination to keep first families contented and comfortable has been exhibited in hundreds of ways. Plumber Howard Arrington was proud of using his metalworking skills to build the elaborate stand for Tricia Nixon's wedding cake. Preston Bruce, who was a doorman from the Eisenhower through the Ford administrations, liked to say that people had only to visit once before he could greet them by name the second time around.

All these men and women are imbued with the same dedication that my favorite among them, Alonzo Fields, epitomized when he said in an interview at the age of ninety-two: "I never felt like a servant to a man. I felt I was a servant to my government, to my country."

There it is again, backstairs as well as frontstairs: glory.

Questions for Discussion

1. What job skills does a chief usher need?

2. What problems occurred when presidents had to pay for the expense of running the White House?

3. Why does it take so many people to run the residential area of the White House?

FDR looks underdressed beside his royal houseguest, King George VI of England. The king and his wife, Queen Elizabeth, stayed at the White House in 1939. Credit: AP/Wide World photos

Bed, Breakfast, and Beyond

THE WHITE HOUSE has no shortage of guest rooms. I've stayed in a couple of them and I can assure you they're the equal of anything you'll find in the world's best hotels. More to the point, every one of them is steeped in history.

The most famous of the White House guest rooms, the Lincoln Bedroom, is on the southeast side of the second floor. It is highly unlikely that Lincoln ever sought repose in the elaborately carved rosewood bed that is the centerpiece of the room, although it was bought during his administration. Mary Lincoln originally put it in the northwest bedroom (where the Prince of Wales stayed when he visited President James Buchanan in 1860). Theodore Roosevelt, with his strong sense of history, had it moved into his own bedroom. Calvin Coolidge also slept in it, but after the Coolidges departed Lou Hoover moved it back to the Prince of Wales Room. She added a suite of parlor furniture that was supposedly owned by Lincoln and rechristened the room the Lincoln Bedroom.

That first Lincoln Bedroom remained in the northwest corner during President Franklin D. Roosevelt's administration. One of its longtime tenants was FDR's close friend and adviser Louis Howe. Some years earlier it had been the room where Grover Cleveland's daughter, Esther, was born and where TR's daughter, Alice, was operated on for appendicitis. Some years later it became my sitting room after another history-minded president, Harry S Truman, aided and abetted by his wife, Bess, moved the furniture to its present location and installed other pieces of Victoriana from the White House storerooms to create what is essentially a shrine to our sixteenth president. At least that's the official story.

The truth of the matter is I started the whole thing. Before we moved into the White House, Mother and I made an inspection tour. We had no trouble selecting the pair of rooms on the second floor that would be my bailiwick. The space was perfect, but the decor left a lot to be desired. (I don't think I used the word *hideous*, but I may have. You have to remember I was only twenty-one.)

In any case, I made it clear that the dark, clunky furniture that was cluttering up my future sitting room had to go. Preferably as far away as possible. Happily, Mother agreed with me. She took up the matter with Dad and the result was the present, and now famous, Lincoln Bedroom at the opposite end of the White House.

II

The second most famous White House guest room is also one of the prettiest: the Queens' Bedroom, which is just across the hall from the Lincoln Bedroom. This was the president's secretary's bedroom when the job was a live-in post. During the Lincoln administration it was shared by John Hay and John George Nicolay—and I'll bet any amount of money it would never have been called pretty.

The room was converted into a guest room after the White House renovation of 1902. It became known as the Rose Room because the curtains and bed hangings were in shades of red, rose, and white. The Rose Room was rechristened in 1942 after a parade of royal refugees bedded down there. Among them: Queens Wilhelmina and Juliana of the Netherlands, Queen Frederika of Greece, Queen Sonya of Norway, Queen Elizabeth II of Great Britain, and her daughter, Princess Anne.

Queen Elizabeth II made her first visit to the White House during the Eisenhower administration in 1957. (She had previously visited Washington as Princess Elizabeth and stayed with Mother and Dad at Blair House.) For Mrs. Eisenhower, the queen's visit was the high point of her husband's presidency and the Queens' Bedroom became almost sacred territory. When Jack Kennedy was elected to the presidency, Jackie made a study of the White House floor plan to see which rooms they could use while the family quarters were being redecorated. "Please put me in the Queens' Room," she told Chief Usher J. B. West, "and my husband will stay in the Lincoln Bedroom."

West passed the word along to the White House staff but when Inauguration Day dawned and the departing first lady read in the papers that her successor would sleep in the Queens' Bedroom, she was quite perturbed. Mrs. Eisenhower thought the Queens' Bedroom should be reserved solely for queens. Jackie didn't qualify.

III

The visit of King George VI and Queen Elizabeth of England in June of 1939 was a momentous occasion. It was the first time a British monarch had set foot in the former colonies. The royal couple came at President Franklin Roosevelt's invitation—an effort on FDR's part to send a signal to Adolf Hitler that the two countries had a special relationship that could lead to trouble if Hitler decided to declare war on England.

The imminent arrival of these ultimate royals touched off a frenzy of activity in the White House. Rugs and draperies were replaced or dry-cleaned and the staff waxed floors and dusted furniture until everything gleamed to housekeeper Henrietta Nesbitt's satisfaction.

The king and queen spent a mere forty-four hours in the White House and, as you might expect, they behaved like proper houseguests. Their servants, however, were a different story. They ensconced themselves on the third floor and proceeded to treat the staff as if they were their servants. They demanded menus so they could order their meals as if they were in a hotel and haughtily explained that in Buckingham Palace they had their own servants to tend to their needs. Needless to say, this did not sit well with their counterparts in the former colonies. Chief Usher Howell Crim had to use all the diplomacy he could muster to avert a second American revolution.

IV

When Winston Churchill came to visit Franklin D. Roosevelt in 1941, shortly after the United States entered World War II, he stayed in the Rose Room. Churchill, who could easily qualify as the houseguest from hell, tried a couple of other rooms before consenting to sleep in the one that had been assigned to him.

The British prime minister's visit was shrouded in secrecy. A few days after Pearl Harbor, President Roosevelt asked his wife for a list of the people who were coming to the White House over Christmas but gave no indication of why he wanted to know. Not until December 22 did Eleanor discover the reason for the president's query. That day, FDR casually announced that Churchill would arrive around nightfall. The secrecy had been necessary to guarantee Mr. Churchill's safety.

When the British leader arrived, complete with cigar, he found the Roosevelts ready to offer him and his entourage tea in the West Hall on the second floor. "But they preferred more stimulating refreshments," Mrs. Roosevelt noted.

Churchill's preferences continued to be at odds with his host's and hostess's. FDR was inclined to go to bed early and rise at a reasonable hour. Churchill was used to working until three A.M. and sleeping late. Eleanor Roosevelt reported that it took "Franklin several days to catch up on his sleep after Mr. Churchill left."

The prime minister made several visits to the White House, often staying as long as two or three weeks. He was an unpredictable and demanding guest. A team of White House staffers had to be assigned to get him the food and drink that he might ask for at any time. He also tended to take baths at odd hours and to rush up and down the corridors in his dressing gown.

In his memoirs, Churchill claimed that his and FDR's "work patterns coincided." They both were in the habit of doing "much of our work in bed," so they frequently visited each other's bedrooms to discuss outstanding problems. One of these visits produced a memorable scene. FDR unceremoniously pushed open Churchill's door and wheeled himself into the room to find the prime minister in the altogether. Churchill gave him a cheerful grin and said: "You see, Mr. President, I have nothing to hide!"

On another evening, Churchill decided his room was overheated and tried to open one of the White House windows. The window, which probably hadn't been opened in decades, resisted. The prime minister kept at it with mighty grunts— and suddenly felt an excruciating pain in his chest. He summoned an aide, who in turn summoned a doctor, who told the great man he had strained his heart, and if he wasn't more careful, he could become the war's best-known casualty. Thereafter, when a window needed opening, the PM called on the White House staff.

The English leader's 1941 visit added a profoundly touching dimension to that first Christmas of World War II. The traditional community Christmas tree was set up on the South Lawn and an enormous crowd gathered behind the iron fence to watch the lighting. They cheered when the tree came aglow. Both leaders gave brief speeches from the South Portico. Churchill's talk summed up the struggle against Hitler in a few unforgettable words:

Let the children have their night of fun and laughter. Let the gifts of Father Christmas delight their play. Let us grown-ups share to the full in their unstinted pleasures before we turn again to the stern task and the formidable years that lie before us, resolved that by our sacrifice and daring, these same children shall not be robbed of their inheritance or denied their right to live in a free and decent world.

Deeply moved, the crowd began singing Christmas carols. Those who were there remembered the scene as one of the most unforgettable moments of their lives. It remains an imperishable part of the White House's glory—and more than made up for Churchill's deficiencies as a houseguest.

V

If there had been a Lincoln Bedroom back in 1824, one of its denizens definitely would have been the Marquis de Lafayette. President James Monroe had invited the Revolutionary War hero to cross the Atlantic to help the country celebrate the fiftieth anniversary of the American Revolution.

Lafayette spent the year after his arrival traveling through all twenty-four states and being fêted at dinners and balls in almost every town he passed through. By the time the old warrior returned to Washington in the summer of 1825, James Monroe was no longer in office. The marquis, dressed in his Continental Army uniform, was greeted at the White House by President John Quincy Adams, and invited to stay for as long as he pleased.

First Lady Louisa Catherine Adams was appalled. It meant

she had to turn most of her family out of their beds to accommodate Lafayette and his party. She also had to find room for the staggering amount of luggage they brought with them, much of it gifts collected on their grand tour. One item that added to Louisa's consternation was a live alligator. The creature and the rest of the booty were stored in the East Room while the marquis enjoyed the final phase of his triumphal tour.

On September 6, 1825, Lafayette's sixty-eighth birthday, President Adams gave a farewell dinner to the nation's guest in the State Dining Room. The table was as splendid as the White House steward could make it. The speeches rang with patriotic fervor. At one point, the two men were so carried away, they burst into tears and embraced. The president summed up the meaning of the grand occasion in his closing words:

"We shall always look upon you as belonging to us. . . . You are ours . . . by that tie of love, stronger than death, which has linked your name for the endless ages of time with the name of Washington."

VI

In 1901, Theodore Roosevelt's secretary released the following statement to the press: "Booker T. Washington of Tuskegee, Alabama, dined with the president last evening." Washington was a distinguished educator and author of the popular book *Up from Slavery*.

Across the country, especially in the South, headlines erupted in dozens of newspapers. With them came angry editorials, denouncing Roosevelt for daring to cross the "color line." The incident was a dismaying example of American racism in full, ugly bloom. Roosevelt had no large agenda in mind when he issued the invitation. He had simply heard Washington was in town and invited him to dinner, as he invited many other celebrities he wanted to meet. He also wanted to "show some respect to a man whom I cordially esteem as a good citizen and a good American." Roosevelt was finding out very early in his presidency how outspoken about certain issues the public could be. He never invited Washington or any other black American again.

Almost thirty years later, a courageous first lady, Lou Hoover, made another attempt to bring racial equality to the White House and found herself in similar hot water. She invited Mrs. Oscar DePriest, wife of an African-American congressman from Chicago, to the White House for tea.

Southern newspapers accused the first lady of "desecrating" the White House. The Texas legislature passed a resolution denouncing her. Sulfurous letters cascaded into the White House mail room. But Lou Hoover stood her ground. After carefully screening the other guests she had invited to the tea, she decided to split the group in half. The women who said they would be pleased to meet Mrs. DePriest were invited to one party, the naysayers to the second.

Years later, Herbert Hoover recalled that the incident had left his wife feeling wounded and appalled. But the president showed that he, too, had the right stuff. He coolly invited Dr. Robert R. Moton, Booker T. Washington's successor as president of the Tuskegee Institute, to have lunch with him a few months later.

VII

I don't have any exact figures but I'm willing to bet that World War II produced the greatest number of VIP White House sleepovers of all time. Security concerns made it advisable for FDR to confer with world leaders at the mansion and their conferences were more easily arranged, and less subject to scrutiny by the press, if the leaders stayed there, too.

The White House logbooks of the era list, among others, the king of Greece, the king of Yugoslavia, the president of the Philippines, the president of Peru, and the prime contender for Winston Churchill's title of houseguest from hell: Madame Chiang Kai-shek. The imperious and temperamental wife of China's embattled Nationalist leader, General Chiang Kai-shek, Madame Chiang was a Wellesley graduate who spoke excellent English and was her husband's partner in political and diplomatic affairs. She was also as willful as any blueblood in her expectations and demands.

Madame Chiang refused to sleep twice on the same sheets. Even when she retired for a brief nap, which she did several times a day, she wanted the entire bed changed. She brought along her own silk sheets, which had to be washed by hand and stitched into the heavy quilted bag she had also brought with her. Howell Crim, the chief usher, gave Madame Chiang a secret nickname: the China Doll. Other members of the staff called her Mrs. Generalissimo, because of the way she ordered them around.

Madame traveled with an entourage of forty. Some of them were given rooms on the third floor, others slept at the Chinese embassy. On the second floor, beds were found for

Madame's personal maid; her nephew and bodyguard, Mr. Kung; and a second nephew also named Kung.

As it turned out, the second Mr. Kung's clothes and haircut were deceptive. A valet who was sent upstairs to help him unpack came flying back to Chief Usher Crim's office to report in horror: "Your Mr. Kung is a girl!"

Miss Kung proved to be as much of a pain as her famous aunt. She not only made demands, she delivered them directly to the first lady. An exasperated Eleanor Roosevelt finally called the chief usher's office: "Mr. Crim," she said, "will you please explain to Miss Kung that she is to call you if she needs anything? She pops into my room a dozen times a day!"

Apparently the chief usher was not high enough in rank for Miss Kung. She transferred her complaints to the State Department, who solved the problem by moving her to a suite at the Mayflower Hotel.

Madame Chiang stayed at the White House more than once. She got along well with the president and she was an effective spokesperson for her country, but the only good thing the staff could say about her was that she was a very generous tipper.

VIII

During Franklin D. Roosevelt's administration, the White House had a number of more or less permanent houseguests. In May 1940, FDR was meeting with his closest adviser, Harry Hopkins, and invited him to stay for dinner. Hopkins became ill during the meal and FDR offered him a bed for the night. Three years later, Hopkins was still using it. His young daughter, Diana, whose mother had recently died, was given a bedroom on the third floor, adding another member to the household.

Harry Hopkins's room was one of the state guest rooms on the southeast side of the house, which later became the Lincoln Bedroom. When the Hopkinses moved to a house in Georgetown in 1943, the Roosevelts' daughter, Anna Boettiger, and her family took over their quarters.

A great many of Eleanor Roosevelt's houseguests were women she had met in the course of working on the various causes she supported. I'm sure the women were all very highminded but at least one of them had a dark side. The guest, who shall remain nameless because the teller of the tale, Alonzo Fields, was too discreet to reveal it, was having trouble closing her suitcase and asked one of the maids to do it while she went down to breakfast.

The maid had to rearrange the woman's clothes, and in the course of repacking them she discovered a fourteen-inch silver tray that had been bought for the White House in 1898 and bore the inscription "The President's House."

The maid called Fields and asked him what she should do about it. "Maybe Mrs. Roosevelt gave the tray to her," the maid suggested. "Should I tell the chief usher?"

"Don't tell anyone," Fields advised. "Just give it to me and I'll take it back to the kitchen."

He knew that Mrs. Roosevelt could not possibly have given the woman the tray, because it didn't belong to her. It belonged to the White House.

The maid was still concerned. Suppose the woman discovered the tray was not in her bag and wanted to know what happened to it?

Fields laughed and said, "The lady will never question you about this, and if she ever returns as a guest she will be ashamed to look you in the eye."

I'm sure that's true, but I'm also sure that if the woman ever returned as a guest, Fields kept an extra sharp eye on the silver.

IX

These days, when someone does something remarkable, he or she may be invited to the White House for a handshake and a photo op with the president, but that's usually about as far as it goes. The world moved at a slower pace back in 1931, which explains why a sixteen-year-old boy from Kiowa County, Colorado, was able to spend four full days at the White House as a guest of President and Mrs. Herbert Hoover.

The boy, Bryan Untiedt, had become a national hero for saving the lives of a group of younger children when they were trapped in a school bus during a blizzard. He had kept them awake and moving to prevent them from freezing to death until they were finally rescued thirty hours later.

Whoever made the arrangements for Bryan's visit to the White House had neglected to tell Mrs. Hoover. She was dismayed to discover that he was due to arrive on the same day as the king and queen of Siam. Not very convenient. On the other hand, the White House has coped with far worse crises.

A car was dispatched to Union Station and Bryan, with a Secret Service man for an escort, was driven to 1600 Pennsylvania Avenue. Instead of the mountain of luggage that most

White House visitors bring, he carried only a cardboard suitcase tied with string and an inexpensive Brownie camera.

Bryan was taken up to the second floor where Mrs. Hoover waited to greet him. In spite of the royal visitors who were expected two hours later, she sat down and chatted with him for several minutes. After a while, Bryan was shown to one of the guest rooms and in keeping with White House custom, a valet was sent to help him unpack. It hardly seemed necessary. The suitcase contained only a few items of clothing and not much else.

Before long, one of the president's secretaries showed up and escorted Bryan to the Oval Office where he had a lengthy chat with the president. Hoover had two sons of his own and he and Bryan got along splendidly.

Lou Hoover asked two women friends who were also staying at the White House to take Bryan for a ride around Washington. They were almost mobbed by photographers when they returned. Bryan was hot copy. But the Hoovers would not allow him to be interviewed. Can you imagine any recent president passing up a chance to get on the evening news with this appealing young hero? I find myself admiring the Hoovers' approach. They were not trying to exploit the boy. They only wanted to reward him for his courage.

The frustrated news hawks reported Bryan was hobnobbing with the king and queen of Siam. On the contrary, he never even saw them unless he peeked out the window of his room, which was just over the North Portico. The Hoovers made sure he did not read these embarrassing articles.

At lunch that day, Bryan sat at the president's right hand, the place of honor. He spent the next three days sightseeing and making good use of his camera. He played with the

Hoovers' grandchildren, romped with their dogs, and shopped for souvenirs to take home to his family. He also had several more chats with Mr. Hoover, sitting in the big armchair in his study, feeling completely at home in the President's House.

X

I don't know about you, but I found Bryan Untiedt's story uniquely American—and deeply moving. It could have happened in no other country in the world but the United States of America. I like to think the President's House, where democracy and power so mysteriously blend, had a lot to do with making it possible.

Questions for Discussion

1. Why was Lafayette's visit to the White House such an emotional occasion?

2. Should the public have anything to say about who is invited to the White House?

3. Why did Franklin D. Roosevelt have so many house-guests?

☆　☆　☆

President and Mrs. Theodore Roosevelt with their six rambunctious children (left to right): Quentin, Theodore Jr., Archibald, Alice, Kermit, and Ethel. Credit: Library of Congress

☆ 10 ☆

Growing Up Under Glass

THERE ARE PLENTY of perks to being the child of a president. One of my favorites was having my own car and driver. Another was the White House movie theater, where I could request any film I wanted. Also on the list: meeting, and being fussed over by some of the greatest figures of the twentieth century; having the best seats in the house at the theater, opera, or ballet; traveling by private plane or train; and receiving an incredible number of fabulous gifts.

Was there a trade-off for all these perks? You bet there was. I couldn't go anywhere without a Secret Service agent in tow; I had to learn to say as little as possible when reporters were around; and, most annoying of all, I had to accept the fact that I was public property. Not only did everyone in the world feel entitled to know all the details of my life, but there were any number of people, both in and out of the media, who felt free to comment on my appearance. My nose was "crooked" and ought to be "fixed." I had "heavy" legs. I was "immature." I was too "mature." And so it went, on and on. A few of the comments gave me a good laugh. I learned to ignore the rest, especially the ones that came from people who would never, under any circumstances, say a good word about Harry S Truman or anyone connected to him.

From reading about, and talking to, other presidential progeny, I realize that although our experiences of living in the White House are similar in many ways, they are also quite different. Anyone who has spent any part of his or her growing-up years at 1600 Pennsylvania Avenue has a highly personal set of memories, some good, some not so good, and, for an unfortunate few, some absolutely dreadful.

II

When John F. Kennedy moved into the White House at the beginning of 1961, America had its dream first family: a young and handsome president, with an even younger and strikingly attractive wife, an adorable three-year-old daughter, and an infant son born on November 25, 1960, less than two weeks after his father's election.

The Kennedy children, Caroline and John Jr., were the youngest occupants of the White House since Grover Cleveland's children toddled the halls. They quickly became its star attractions. The media were so hungry for news of Caroline that one editor snapped at his Washington correspondent, "Never mind that stuff about Laos. What did Caroline do today?"

Being at an age where she was completely unself-conscious, Caroline provided more than a few newsworthy items. She once wandered into a press conference wearing her nightie and a pair of her mother's high heels. Another time, when a reporter asked where her father was, Caroline said, "He's upstairs with his shoes and socks off doing nothing."

Jacqueline Kennedy set up a nursery school for Caroline and about a dozen other youngsters in the third-floor solarium. The parents shared the cost of hiring a teacher and purchasing blocks, paints, a sandbox, and other school supplies. Jackie also installed a small playground on the South Lawn, which the president could see from his office. When he wanted to take a break from work, he would step outside and clap his hands and the children would come running over for a visit.

Not long after the playground was installed, Jackie realized that it was visible from the street. When the tour bus drivers started making it a stop on their schedule, she had a line of rhododendrons planted along the fence to block the view.

Jacqueline Kennedy was so determined to maintain her children's privacy that she requested her husband not be photographed with them too often. Jack didn't always comply. Knowing how politicians love to get their pictures taken with children, as well as how cute these particular children were, I can understand why.

Like many little girls, and a few little boys, Caroline liked to talk on the phone. She was on the line with her father one day chatting about the gifts she was hoping to get for Christmas. In the course of their conversation, she told him how much she wished she could call up Santa Claus and tell him exactly what she wanted.

The president promised to see what he could do. He called the White House switchboard and asked one of the operators to take Caroline's call and pretend she was answering the phone at Santa Claus's workshop at the North Pole. Then the president put in a call to the nursery and told Caroline he had managed to get through to Santa Claus's workshop.

Caroline got on the line. Her face fell when she was told that Santa wasn't home but she brightened up when she discovered that she was talking to Mrs. Santa Claus, who offered to take a message for her husband. Caroline rattled off a long list of toys for herself and John and hung up thoroughly convinced that she had been connected to the North Pole.

In his early months at the White House, young John Kennedy spent many hours napping in his carriage on the Truman balcony. He was too young to get into mischief then, but he made up for it when he reached the toddler stage.

John was fascinated by the White House helicopter and loved to take it on family trips to Camp David or Glen Ora, the Kennedys' Virginia estate. He refused to accept the fact that his father sometimes used it for other purposes. John would be all smiles as he watched the helicopter land on the South Lawn then burst into tears when his father climbed in and took off without him. Onlookers sometimes thought he was crying because his father was leaving, but it was really because John wasn't getting a ride.

The Truman balcony provided Caroline and John with a perfect vantage point from which to observe the arrival and departure of VIP visitors and the ceremonies to welcome heads of state. One day while the television crews were setting up their equipment to film the arrival of Marshal Josip Broz Tito of Yugoslavia, John dropped one of his toy guns. It fell through the railing on the balcony and landed in the tangle of wires below. A cameraman got a shot of the falling gun and it was later inserted into a newsclip of Tito's speech. One network reported that the gun had landed on Tito's head; another account had it beaning one of the soldiers in the presidential honor guard. Neither story was true, of course, but it made good copy and that's all the reporters cared about.

Caroline and John F. Kennedy, Jr.'s childhood days at 1600 Pennsylvania Avenue ended abruptly when their father was assassinated on November 22, 1963. Plans were already in the works for the children's birthday parties. John's third birthday was on November 25 and Caroline's sixth on November 27. The parties were canceled but the children had a combined celebration about a week later, the only happy event during those sad weeks when their mother was preparing to move out of the White House.

Isn't it ironic that John, who was so entranced with flying as a little boy, died when the private plane he was piloting crashed into the sea off Cape Cod in the summer of 1999?

III

Over the years, there have been very few presidents' children as young as Caroline and John F. Kennedy, Jr. Most first offspring have had either one or both feet out of the nest for the simple reason that by the time most men get to the White House, they are fifty-something or more. Dad was a few weeks shy of sixty-one.

Grover Cleveland is the wild card in all this. A forty-seven-year-old bachelor when he was inaugurated for his first term in 1884, he surprised everyone by marrying his twenty-one-year-old ward, Frances Folsom, two years later. The Clevelands' first child, Ruth, was born in New York City, where her parents had moved after her father lost his bid for a second term.

He was reelected the following year and returned to the White House on March 4, 1893, precisely four years after he left.

Two-year-old Ruth promptly became the nation's darling. She was so popular that the candy bar, the Baby Ruth, was named in her honor. By the time Cleveland's second term ended in 1896, Ruth had two little sisters, Esther and Marion. Esther was the first, and only, child of a president to be born in the White House. Marion arrived while her parents were at their summer home on Cape Cod.

Grover Cleveland had always cherished his privacy and given short shrift to the press. Now that he had three young daughters, he became more determined than ever to keep his family out of the limelight. The Clevelands bought a home, Woodley, in a rural section of Washington and the family spent as much time there as possible.

In 1962, a writer for *The New Yorker* talked to Esther Cleveland Bosanquet about her memories of the White House. She recalled several things: a huge Christmas tree with heaps of toys underneath, the Easter egg rolling on the lawn, and visiting her father in his study in the evenings. "I remember very vividly that he once let me dip my fingers in his inkwell and make big blobs on his papers."

In 1929, Marion Cleveland Amen was invited to the White House by Lou Henry Hoover. The visit triggered no memories until she visited the family quarters on the second floor. There she was struck by the strong, slightly musty scent of roses. Later, she asked her mother if there was anything unusual about the smell of the second floor. "Yes," her mother replied, "that one floor had the smell of an old house by the sea, a musty scent, overlaid with roses."

IV

Not until Abraham Lincoln became president in 1860 did the White House have honest-to-goodness kids in residence. The Lincolns' oldest son, Robert, was a dignified Harvard freshman, but his younger brothers, ten-year-old Willie and seven-year-old Tad (whose real name was Thomas), kept things hopping at 1600 Pennsylvania Avenue.

In the course of exploring their new home, Willie and Tad discovered the bell system that was used for summoning the White House servants. They also figured out how to make all the bells ring at once, which caused chaos when footmen and housemaids rushed to respond, only to discover that no one had called them.

Willie and Tad became friends with the sons of a Washington judge, Horatio Taft, who lived nearby. The boys—Horatio Jr., who was known as Bud; and Halsey, whose nickname was Holly—often visited the White House, and occasionally all four boys could be found wrestling with the president on the parlor floor.

When Willie died of typhoid fever in February 1862, Tad was as downhearted as his parents. His father did everything he could think of to cheer him up, including buying him a pair of goats. The president knew Tad's high spirits had returned when he hitched the goats to an upside-down chair to make a chariot and went tearing through the East Room. The sight startled a group of women visitors and sent the president, who was watching from the hall outside, into a fit of laughter.

Tad's other misdeeds included locking his father in Lafayette Park, and standing in front of the White House waving a Confederate flag while his father was reviewing Union troops.

I wish I could report that Tad developed into a charming and fun-loving adult but he died of pneumonia at the age of eighteen, adding still further to his widowed mother's enormous burden of grief.

V

By the time Ulysses S. Grant became president in 1869, the White House and its occupants found themselves in full view of the public eye. This new focus developed in tandem with the growth of the popular press. As more and more women became educated, newspapers and magazines started catering to their interests. Articles about the chief executive and his family became a staple in the women's magazines of the era.

The Grants did not object to all this attention. But they tried to keep it under control. Julia Grant had the south grounds closed so the children could enjoy the White House backyard without being gawked at by strangers.

There were four children in the Grant family. The oldest, Fred, was at West Point. The second, Ulysses Jr., nicknamed Buck, went off to boarding school not long after his father's election. That left only thirteen-year-old Nellie and ten-year-old Jesse living at the White House full-time.

As the only girl, Nellie was her parents' pet and they could not resist spoiling her. Realizing that she was in need of more discipline than she was getting at home, they decided to send her to Miss Porter's School in Farmington, Connecticut. The president took her there himself lest "Julia cry and bring her back."

Grant had barely returned to the White House when a telegram arrived from Nellie demanding to come home. Her parents urged her to stay longer, assuring her that she would get used to the school, but Nellie was adamant. By Thanksgiving, she was back in Washington, where she spent most of her time going to parties and driving around town in her phaeton, a horse-drawn version of today's convertible.

Jesse gave his parents fewer headaches. He was one of those boys who are always involved in some kind of hobby. He had a microscope and a camera but his favorite instrument was a telescope that was a gift from one of Ulysses S. Grant's admirers. Jesse set it up on the White House roof and he and his father became amateur astronomers, studying the planets and constellations each night until Julia Grant had to send someone up to remind them that it was time for Jesse to go to bed.

Another of Jesse's hobbies was stamp collecting. Once he and one of his cousins, Baine Dent, saved up the astronomical sum of five dollars and sent away to a Boston company for some foreign stamps they had seen advertised in a newspaper. Weeks went by and the stamps never arrived. Finally, Jesse consulted his good friend Kelly, a member of the Washington police force assigned to the White House.

Kelly advised young Jesse to speak to his father about the matter. Jesse did and the president responded by asking him what exactly his son expected him to do about it.

"I thought you might have the secretary of state or the secretary of war, or Kelly, write a letter," Jesse replied.

"A matter of this importance requires consideration," the president told him. "Suppose you come to the cabinet meeting tomorrow and we will take the matter up there."

When the problem was presented to the cabinet members,

both the secretary of state and the secretary of war offered to intervene, but after some discussion it was agreed that a warning from Officer Kelly would carry the most weight.

And so, "the sweat standing out on his forehead, his great fingers gripping the pen," Officer Kelly wrote the following letter on Executive Mansion stationery:

I am a Capitol Policeman. I can arrest anybody, anywhere, at any time for anything. I want you to send those stamps to Jesse Grant right at once.

Kelly, Capitol policeman

Jesse and Baine got their stamps and then some. "As I remember," Jesse recalled, "that five-dollar assortment exceeded our expectations."

VI

The two presidents who came after Ulysses S. Grant—Rutherford B. Hayes and James A. Garfield—each had five children. The Hayeses' three older sons were born before the Civil War and were pretty well grown by the time their father took office, but their two younger children, nine-year-old Frances, better known as Fanny, and six-year-old Scott, were very much in evidence during their father's presidency.

The Hayeses celebrated their first Thanksgiving in the White House by inviting the secretaries, executive clerks, stenographers, and telegraph operator with their wives and families to dinner. After dinner, the children played blindman's buff in the State Rooms. Another game of blindman's buff was held in the East Room when thirty children, Scott and his guests, celebrated his seventh birthday.

Rutherford and Lucy Hayes often included their children in White House activities. One of Scott's biggest kicks was meeting a delegation of Native Americans who came to plead for their homelands. He was thrilled when the Sioux chief, Red Cloud, patted him on the head and called him a "young brave."

On Memorial Day, Fanny joined her mother and some friends at Arlington National Cemetery to decorate the graves of Civil War soldiers. At Christmas, the children helped their mother distribute gifts to the White House staff, and on Easter Monday they donned their Sunday best and presided over the annual Easter egg roll on the White House lawn.

For many years, this event had been held on Capitol Hill, but in 1878, Congress decided to prohibit public use of the grounds. Unaware of the ban, the children showed up on Easter Monday 1879 and were turned away by the Capitol police. Disappointed and angry, they proceeded down Pennsylvania Avenue to the White House, where President Hayes offered them the use of the South Lawn and created a White House custom that endures to this day.

VII

The largest and liveliest group of children to live at 1600 Pennsylvania Avenue was Theodore Roosevelt's family of six, which included sixteen-year-old Alice, his daughter by his first marriage to Alice Lee, who died in childbirth, and her half brothers and sister, Theodore Jr., fourteen; Kermit, twelve; Ethel, nine; Archibald, seven; and Quentin, four.

The older children, Alice and Ted, might have been expected to be more sedate, but they were not above joining their younger siblings in such antics as sliding down staircases on tin trays borrowed from the kitchen, roller-skating in the East Room, or stilt-walking and bicycle riding through the upstairs halls. Quentin, who liked to go speeding through the house in his wagon, once crashed into a full-length portrait of Lucy Webb Hayes, leaving a hole in the canvas. On another occasion, Quentin and Archie livened up an otherwise ordinary afternoon by following the White House lamplighter around the grounds and turning off the lights as he turned them on.

For the most part, the Roosevelts enjoyed their children's antics, but they were quick to enforce discipline when the occasion demanded. One night, when Quentin had a sleepover for some of his friends—they called themselves the White House gang—the boys sneaked downstairs and peppered a portrait of President Andrew Jackson with spitballs. They finished the job by climbing on chairs and arranging the soggy lumps in designs—three across his forehead, one on each of his coat buttons, blobs on both ears, and another blob on the tip of his nose.

The boys scampered back upstairs and were just drifting off to sleep when the president flung open the door, dragged Quentin from beneath the covers, and whisked him out of the room. The next morning, the gang learned that Q, as they called him, had been forced to remove the spitballs under his father's watchful eye. Nor did the rest of the gang escape.

They were all summoned to the president's office for a stern lecture on respecting public property.

As his siblings went off to boarding school one by one, Quentin and his gang all but took over the White House. They spent hours exploring the mansion from attic to basement and once disrupted the Departments of War and Navy, in their adjacent building, by using mirrors to flash sunbeams into their office windows, almost blinding the staff.

One spring the gang encountered two plumbers working on the fountain on the South Lawn and started pestering them with questions about what they were doing. The men quickly tired of the cross-examination and shooed the boys away, whereupon Quentin led them to a large iron door sunk into the ground behind a clump of evergreens. The boys managed to open the door and turn the key in the massive valve that controlled the flow of water to the fountain. A few minutes later, streams of water came gushing out of the pipes on which the men were sitting. One man was lifted straight off his perch; his coworker slid backward into the empty pool. They both lay sprawled on the bottom while the water from the fountain rose in a graceful arc and thoroughly doused them. The gang members beat a swift retreat and avoided the South Lawn for the next couple of weeks.

Perhaps the gang's worst crime was rolling a giant snowball off the roof of the North Portico. It hit one of the White House policemen squarely on the head and knocked him out. The president, who was just stepping into his carriage, saw the prank and although he tried to control himself, he couldn't resist laughing. Fortunately, only the policeman's dignity was injured, but the gang got yet another presidential lecture along with orders to apologize.

Roosevelt's lectures usually persuaded his children to behave themselves, at least temporarily. The one exception was Alice, who defied her father's attempts at discipline and seemed to delight in finding ways to annoy him. He disapproved of women smoking and forbade her to do it under his roof. Alice made her way up the White House staircases and smoked on the roof. To liven up a particularly dull social event, she once pulled out a cap pistol and started shooting at the startled guests.

As Roosevelt famously said to an old friend, "I can do one of two things. I can be president of the United States or I can control Alice. I cannot possibly do both."

VIII

Calvin Coolidge was sworn in as president of the United States after the sudden death of Warren G. Harding in the early morning hours of August 3, 1923. The new president's sons, John, almost seventeen, and Calvin Jr., fifteen, were not at home that summer and the laconic Coolidge let them find out on their own that they would be moving into the White House.

Calvin Jr. had a summer job harvesting tobacco for which he was paid three dollars and fifty cents a day. When one of his coworkers heard the news, he remarked that if his father were president, he wouldn't be harvesting tobacco. Calvin responded, "If my father were your father, you would."

The following summer, John, who had just graduated from Mercersburg Academy in Mercersburg, Pennsylvania, was in a military training program at Fort Devens, Massachusetts, while Calvin Jr., who was on vacation from Mercersburg, remained at home. The 1924 Republican convention met in June and nominated Coolidge to run for president in his own right and he was spending the summer in the White House preparing for the campaign.

One day toward the end of June, young Calvin was playing tennis without any socks on. With his bare feet rubbing directly against his tennis shoes, he soon developed a blister on his right toe. He paid no attention to it until it started to hurt. When he mentioned the pain to his parents, they sent him to the White House doctor who saw that the blister had become infected and ordered the young man to bed.

By the Fourth of July, the infection had turned into blood poisoning. Calvin's temperature rose and he drifted in and out of consciousness. By July 6 the doctors were holding out little hope. On the slim chance that surgery might help, he was taken by ambulance to Walter Reed Hospital, where, in his feverish state, he tossed and turned and seemed to have the impression he was leading a charge of troops into battle. Suddenly he murmured "We surrender" and fell into a coma. He died the following evening.

Some weeks later a newsman who had known Coolidge when he was active in Massachusetts politics called at the White House to express his sympathy. "I am sorry," he said. "Calvin was a good boy."

Coolidge swiveled around in his chair and stared out the windows of the Oval Office for several minutes. "You know," he finally responded, "I sit here thinking of it, and I just can't believe it has happened." The president was in tears as he repeated the last sentence. "I just can't believe it has happened."

Later, writing in his autobiography about the loss of his son,

Coolidge said, "When he went, the power and the glory of the Presidency went with him."

IX

Chelsea Clinton was the second young woman in history to be the only child of the president of the United States. I was the first. In some ways, our experiences are not really comparable. I was twenty-one when we moved to the White House; Chelsea was only twelve. But there are a few parallels.

With no siblings to share the limelight, we both came in for an inordinate amount of attention—good and bad. My parents made sure I didn't let being a first daughter throw me, and from everything I've seen and heard, Bill and Hillary Clinton were just as careful not to let Chelsea get carried away by it, either.

In spite of the myriad problems with which the Clintons had to cope—scandals, investigations, impeachment— Chelsea's needs were not neglected. Not only did she get through eight years in the White House with a reasonable amount of privacy, she seems to have had a very good time.

Chelsea had pizza parties in the State Dining Room and sleepovers on the third floor of the White House with her classmates. When she graduated, Bill Clinton was the speaker, joining two other presidents—Lyndon Johnson and Theodore Roosevelt—who delivered commencement addresses at their daughters' schools. Knowing her father's tendency to be long-winded, Chelsea warned him in advance to be brief.

Jenna and Barbara Bush, the latest presidential daughters to occupy the White House, are also the first set of twins. That's had the media panting for stories, but so far the Bushes have followed the policy the Clintons adopted with Chelsea: No comments, period.

The Bush daughters were both in college, just as I was when my father became president. Back then, the reporters were all over Dad's press secretary, Charlie Ross, begging him to let them interview me. Even if I had wanted to hold a press conference (which I didn't) and even if my parents would have let me (which they wouldn't), I didn't have anything to say.

Charlie, smart, wonderful man that he was, was as anxious as my parents were to protect my privacy, but having been a newspaperman himself, he knew he couldn't hold the reporters at bay indefinitely, so he came up with a clever solution.

"We'll let them follow you around for one whole day," he said, "and they'll soon realize that there isn't anything to write about."

Charlie, as usual, was right. After clearing the matter with the university administration, he told the reporters they could follow me around the campus of George Washington University for a day and see how I spent my time.

If any of those journalists thought they were going to come away with a great story, they must have been pretty disappointed. They spent most of the day shuttling from one classroom to another and sitting through courses in history and government. It quickly dawned on them that I was leading a life that was much like that of any other college student and, as Charlie had foreseen, they decided to leave me alone—at least until I graduated and did something newsworthy on my own.

X

When I chatted with Chelsea Clinton during a visit my husband and I made to the White House in 1993, one of the key questions she asked me was "Did you enjoy living here?"

My answer was an unqualified yes. Living in the White House is a unique privilege, and for anyone who is as interested in American history as I am, it provides unbeatable insights into the workings of the government and the day-to-day lives of the men and women who shaped this country.

The biggest lesson I learned from the experience is that the White House is not the real world, and when you walk out the door and the next president and his family walk in, it's all over. No more household staff ready to press a skirt or sew on a button in an emergency, no more unending supplies of chocolate ice cream—my favorite—in the freezer, no more special treatment everywhere you go.

Unless you've learned to put the experience in perspective, it can be a terrible letdown. I have to confess that after a year or two in my role as first daughter, I got a little full of myself, which was against the rules in the Truman household. My father saw what was happening and after I had spent a weekend in Washington—by this time, I was living in New York—he sat down and wrote me a letter. The gist of his message was not to get carried away by the White House aura. "Keep your balance," he said. "Do not let the glamour get you."

If I were the advice-giving type, I'd pass that along to every young person who faces the challenge of living in the White House.

Questions for Discussion

1. Why might a young person enjoy living in the White House?

2. What would be some of the drawbacks?

3. Can presidents' children lead normal lives?

FRANK LESLIE'S ILLUSTRATED NEWSPAPER

NEW YORK, JUNE 6, 1874.

THE WEDDING AT THE WHITE HOUSE

Nellie Grant was not the first White House bride, but her wedding was the first to attract public attention. Every detail was reported in the press. Credit: Library of Congress

☆ 11 ☆

Here Come the Brides

DURING THE SEVEN and two-thirds years Dad was in the White House, there was never any shortage of news. Just for openers, we had the dropping of the atomic bomb, the end of World War II, and the beginning of the Korean War. But in the midst of all this, the media was always on the lookout for the really big story: When was I going to get married?

I'm afraid I disappointed them. I didn't get married until 1956—four years after Dad left office. It was another ten years before the reporters finally got the story of their dreams: a White House wedding. But perhaps to make up for the long wait, they got a doubleheader: Luci Johnson's in 1965 and her sister Lynda Bird's two years later.

The Johnsons weren't the first pair of presidential daughters to get married during their father's administration. Two of Woodrow Wilson's three daughters did the same thing. There have been other White House brides as well, but the wedding that occupies a truly unique place in the annals of 1600 Pennsylvania Avenue took place on June 2, 1886. The bride was a twenty-one-year-old beauty from upstate New York named Frances Folsom and the groom was none other than the president himself—crotchety, forty-nine-year-old Grover Cleveland, a lifelong bachelor who supposedly worked so hard he didn't have time for a wife.

II

Grover Cleveland had known Frances Folsom—her family and friends called her Frank—all her life. Her father, Oscar Folsom, had been Cleveland's partner in his Buffalo, New York, law office. When Oscar was killed in a carriage accident in 1875, Cleveland became Frank's legal guardian. She was eleven years old at the time.

It is not clear when he started thinking about a change in their relationship, but by the time Frances was a student at Wells College in Aurora, New York, Cleveland was regularly sending her flowers. After he became president in 1884, the flowers came from the White House conservatory.

Frances graduated from Wells in 1885 and embarked with her mother and her cousin Benjamin Folsom on a tour of Europe. She had already agreed to marry Cleveland. He proposed one night when they were walking together in the East Room during a visit she paid to the White House as the guest of his sister, Rose.

Sometime between that conversation and the time Frances sailed for Europe, the wedding date was set and they agreed to be married at the White House. Frances decided it was the only place they could be sure of having some privacy.

Shortly before the Folsoms were scheduled to return to the

United States, rumors of the president's secret engagement began circulating, but because of the difference in the couple's ages, it was assumed that he was engaged not to Frances, but to her widowed mother.

Toward the end of May, the Folsoms' ship docked in New York. A crowd of reporters was on hand to interview the bride-to-be but there was no sign of her. The president's secretary, Daniel Lamont, had arranged to meet the ship in the harbor, take the Folsoms aboard a government revenue cutter, and whisk them off to their hotel.

By this time the identity of the bride was no longer a mystery. Cleveland had sent handwritten notes to slightly more than two dozen friends inviting them to the ceremony. Meanwhile, the press was using every imaginable form of pressure to be allowed to cover the proceedings, and a small army of would-be gate-crashers were racking their brains for ways to get past the guards. One enterprising fellow offered band leader John Philip Sousa fifty dollars to let him don a uniform and pose as a triangle player in the Marine Band.

Frances wore a gown of ivory satin with a fifteen-foot train, but aside from the elaborate gown, it was a very simple wedding. The ceremony was held in the Blue Room and the president entered the room with his bride on his arm. The twenty-eight guests stood in a semicircle during the brief ceremony while outside, cannon boomed in an official salute. Church bells rang out all over Washington and in many other cities as well. Afterward the guests adjourned to the State Dining Room for refreshments.

Frances and Grover Cleveland not only enjoyed an extremely happy marriage, but Frances turned out to be the most popular first lady since Dolley Madison.

III

Alice Roosevelt Longworth was one of my favorite Washingtonians. She had a sharp eye and an even sharper wit, plus a gift for being delightfully outrageous. I always liked the inscription on the pillow she kept on her living room sofa: "If you haven't got anything nice to say about anybody, come sit next to me."

"The other Washington Monument," as Alice was sometimes called, was a commanding figure on the D.C. social scene long before the Trumans got to Washington and long after we left. She died in 1980 at the age of ninety-six, almost seventy-eight years after she swooped into the public eye by becoming the first presidential daughter to make her debut in the White House.

In those days, "coming out" was a signal, not unlike the sound of the starter's pistol in a race. If you didn't get married within the next two or three years, you were counted among the losers. So, of course, Alice's debut immediately started a wave of speculation about when, where, and, above all, whom she would marry.

Alice tantalized the gossipmongers for three years before she finally said yes to Congressman Nicholas Longworth of Cincinnati, Ohio. Their wedding was to take place in the White House on February 17, 1906.

The always imperious "Princess Alice" had quite a bit to say about the arrangements, but her chief interest was in the gifts. As one White House aide remarked, she would accept anything but a red-hot stove "and will take that if it does not take too long to cool."

No red-hot stoves appeared, but the collection did include mousetraps, bales of hay, feather dusters, and a hogshead of popcorn—all sent by the companies that sold them in hopes of gaining some publicity for their products. To make up for what Alice called the "freak presents," there was a gold snuff box from King Edward VII of England with his miniature set in diamonds on the lid, a $25,000 string of pearls from the people of Cuba, and some bolts of brocade and silk from the dowager empress of China that provided Alice with evening wear for the next few decades.

The wedding took place at noon. Although sketches of the event show the bride marching down the Grand Staircase on her father's arm, according to Alice they actually took the elevator down to the State Dining Room and walked through the main hall to the East Room. The ceremony was performed by the Episcopal bishop of Washington and the guests included Roosevelt family members and personal friends, ambassadors, cabinet members, senators, Supreme Court justices, and the president's favorite hunting guide wearing a frock coat and top hat for the first time in his life.

There were several wedding cakes, including one that was two and a half feet high and topped with a statue of Cupid ringing a silver wedding bell. Alice, who rarely did anything the usual way, cut it with a sword borrowed from Major Charles McCawley of the U.S. Marine Corps, one of the White House military aides.

By four that afternoon, a large crowd had gathered outside the White House, hoping to catch a glimpse of the newlyweds as they left on their honeymoon. There were four different cars parked at various points on the White House grounds. While the crowd was trying to decide which one to keep their eyes on, Nick and Alice went into the Red Room, opened a window, stepped onto the South Portico, and scurried down the steps to a fifth car.

Among those who missed the departure was a movie photographer who had been ordered by his boss to come back with some footage or else. Rather than risk the "or else," the man hired a car and enlisted a look-alike couple to reenact the scene. With the jerky, blurry film of the day, nobody knew the difference.

IV

Among the guests at Alice Roosevelt Longworth's wedding was fifty-year-old Ellen Wrenshall Grant Sartoris, better known as Nellie, who had enjoyed an equally glittering White House wedding thirty-two years earlier.

Nellie was fifteen when her father was elected president. She was beautiful, headstrong, and determined to enjoy every bit of the attention she got from being the president's only daughter. A few years after she resisted her parents' attempt to send her to boarding school, the Grants decided a vacation from the limelight was in order. Some old friends were planning a tour of Europe with their children, and at her parents' suggestion Nellie was invited to join them.

Nellie's European tour turned out to be one long round of party-going—just what her parents had been hoping to get her away from. To top it off, on the return voyage, she met, and fell madly in love with, a young diplomat named Algernon Sartoris, who had just been posted to the British legation in Washington.

Sartoris was rich, good-looking, and well-educated, but in spite of these recommendations, the Grants were less than thrilled with the match. They would have preferred that Nellie marry an American. Moreover, she was only seventeen, and she and Algernon had not known each other long enough to be sure they were making the right choice.

As usual Nellie got her way, although her parents achieved a victory of sorts by making the couple agree to wait a year before announcing their engagement. When the year was up, early in 1874, the announcement was made and preparations for what was later called "one of the most brilliant weddings ever given in the United States" got under way.

The date was set for Thursday, May 21, and the guest list was said to be small. Only 250 invitations were sent out. The wedding was held in the East Room, which had been redecorated the previous summer. The ceremony was brief, and when it was over, everyone adjourned to the State Dining Room for a wedding breakfast that one guest described as being "as elaborate as money and thought could make it."

I wish I could report that Nellie and Algernon lived happily ever after. Unfortunately, Algernon developed a serious drinking problem and Nellie left him to return to the United States with their four children. Algernon died of pneumonia in 1893 at the age of forty-two. Eighteen years later, Nellie married one of her childhood sweethearts, but a few months after the wedding she became seriously ill and remained an invalid until her death in 1922.

V

I used to think my father was overprotective until I read about Woodrow Wilson. When Wilson and his first wife, Ellen, moved into the White House in 1913, their three daughters—Margaret, twenty-six; Jessie, twenty-five; and Eleanor, or Nellie, twenty-three—were all living at home. I have no problem with that. In those days most young women lived with their parents until they got married. But the president was so fond of being surrounded by his family that he would have been quite content if they never set up homes of their own.

Before his election to the presidency in 1912, Wilson had been governor of New Jersey. The family lived in Princeton and Jessie, the middle daughter, an angelic-looking blonde who had graduated Phi Beta Kappa from Goucher College in Baltimore, worked at a settlement house in Philadelphia during the week and returned to Princeton on weekends.

One weekend, a friend of the Wilsons, Blanche Nevin, invited Jessie and Nellie to her country home in Pennsylvania. She also invited her nephew, Francis Bowes Sayre, a recent graduate of Harvard Law School, with an eye to promoting a romance between him and Jessie.

Blanche's matchmaking talents proved to be excellent. Frank and Jessie fell in love at first sight and before long Frank proposed. Since Jessie's father was in the final days of his campaign for the presidency, they agreed not to say anything until after the election.

Jessie's mother, Ellen Wilson, was pretty sure what was going on, but her husband was so preoccupied with the campaign that he didn't have a clue. As he was leaving home one day, he met a young man walking up the steps. The two men smiled and nodded and Wilson later asked his wife who "that nice-looking sandy-haired boy" might be.

"That's Frank Sayre," she replied. "And I think you're going to be his father-in-law."

It took a few weeks for Woodrow Wilson to get used to the idea of losing one of his daughters, but he finally conceded that he was growing to love his prospective son-in-law and that Frank was "almost good enough for Jessie."

Frank and Jessie's engagement was announced the following July and it was agreed that the wedding would take place at the White House on Tuesday, November 25. (The couple insisted on a Tuesday because that was the day Jessie said yes.)

Since the wedding was a private affair, President Wilson let it be known that presents were not to be sent by anyone who wasn't a personal friend of the couple. Theodore Roosevelt had made the same announcement, to no avail. Jessie was inundated with gifts. In addition to the usual collection of "freak presents" as Alice Roosevelt Longworth called them— washtubs, boxes of soap, coal scuttles, and sacks of onions— the list included a fourteen-piece silver service from the Senate, and a diamond necklace and pendant from all but one of the members of the House of Representatives. That gentleman, Congressman Finley H. Gray of Indiana, claimed the gift was "in bad taste" and chose to make a contribution to the poor instead.

The standing rule for White House weddings is that no one is admitted without a ticket. In this case, the one person who forgot his ticket was Frank Sayre. He arrived at the front gate a few hours before the wedding and the guard on duty refused to let him in. Frank identified himself as the groom but the guard was adamant. Anyone could claim to be the groom, he said. Finally, Frank suggested that the guard call his captain. The captain came marching out of his sentry box, listened sternly to Frank's explanation, and with a slight wink, let him in.

VI

Just as one Wilson daughter's wedding was winding down, a second was starting up. After Jessie and her new husband left their wedding reception, the party kept going, thanks to her younger sister Nellie, who loved to dance and kept the Marine Band playing for several hours beyond their agreed-on quitting time.

On the evening of Jessie's wedding her most frequent dance partner was Secretary of the Treasury William Gibbs McAdoo, a widower with six children who was almost fifty years old and a grandfather to boot. McAdoo was tall and handsome with courtly southern manners. His business successes had led to his appointment as vice chairman of the Democratic National Committee, and he and Wilson had become close friends during the 1912 presidential campaign.

By the time Jessie and Frank returned from their honeymoon, Nellie and the secretary of the treasury were seeing quite a bit of each other. One evening when the family was together in the second-floor Oval Room, one of the servants announced the arrival of Secretary McAdoo. The president started to get up and then the servant added, "For Miss Eleanor."

Mac had already proposed once and Nellie had put him off.

When he proposed a second time, she said yes. Nellie's nuptials were smaller and less glittering than Jessie's, partly because Mac had been married before and partly because Nellie's mother, Ellen, had not been feeling well. The ceremony took place in the Blue Room and only about one hundred people were invited.

Nellie returned from her honeymoon to find that her mother's health had deteriorated. Ellen Wilson died in August 1914, leaving her daughters devastated and her husband deeply depressed.

A little more than six months later, Woodrow Wilson met an attractive widow named Edith Bolling Galt and his spirits began to lift. By the end of 1915, another member of the Wilson family got married. This time it was the president, but the wedding took place at Mrs. Galt's home, not at the White House.

VII

After John F. Kennedy's assassination in 1963, Lyndon and Lady Bird Johnson arrived in the White House with two teenaged daughters. At sixteen, Luci was too young for any serious romance, but the gossip columnists quickly discovered that nineteen-year-old Lynda Bird was dating a young navy lieutenant and supposedly wearing his ring. That started a buzz about an impending wedding, but the chatter ended abruptly when the couple broke up a few months later.

As it turned out, Luci beat Lynda Bird to the altar by more than two years. One of her friends, Beth Jenkins, attended Marquette University in Milwaukee, Wisconsin, and in the course of visiting Beth, Luci met a young man named Patrick J. Nugent. Before long, she and Pat were commuting back and forth between Milwaukee and Washington, but the press never caught on—possibly because they were preoccupied with Lynda Bird's love life or maybe it was because Luci's blond wig threw them off the scent.

In the fall of 1965, Luci and Pat made a trip to the LBJ ranch in Johnson City, Texas, to request the president's permission to marry. As soon as the media got wind of their plans, the White House press office was bombarded with questions and requests for details.

Eventually, all—or almost all—was revealed. The wedding was to take place at noon on Saturday, August 6, 1966. The reception would be held at the White House but the ceremony would be performed at the National Shrine of the Immaculate Conception in northeast Washington. Although it was not generally known, Luci had converted to Catholicism, the religion of her fiancé.

Luci insisted that the design of her wedding dress be kept secret until she walked down the aisle. This produced security precautions worthy of a summit conference. The designer, Priscilla of Boston, was met at the airport by the Secret Service, and the dress was hand-carried to the White House and locked in the Lincoln Bedroom. It was taken out, presumably under armed guard, so Luci could wear it for her bridal portrait, but during the photo session no one was allowed to use the elevators or walk through the White House halls until the all clear was sounded.

Luci's wedding day dawned hot and humid—hardly a surprise in a city noted for its sweltering summers. During the ceremony, Lynda Bird, the maid of honor, and two of the bridesmaids almost fainted. Another bridesmaid and the matron of honor did pass out.

Even more noteworthy was the way the perennially impatient father of the bride sat still during the entire eighty-five-minute ceremony. Lady Bird's social secretary, Bess Abell, reported in amazement, "I do not remember him looking at his watch one single time during the service."

The only glitch of the day occurred when someone mistakenly packed Luci's going-away outfit in one of the suitcases she planned to take on her honeymoon. The suitcase was already stowed in the trunk of the getaway car, but Luci refused to leave until the outfit—a deep pink suit with matching turban—was retrieved.

When it was finally found, she changed out of her wedding gown and went down to the South Portico to throw her bouquet, which landed squarely at Lynda Bird's feet. With this last ritual performed, Luci slipped back upstairs, changed out of the pink suit and turban and into an inconspicuous dark dress and a hairpiece that turned her short hair into shoulder-length curls. At last she was ready to depart.

The newlyweds' getaway worked out as planned. Luci and Pat went through the tunnel that connects the White House to the Treasury Building next door. There, a nondescript black sedan was waiting in the basement garage. The couple crouched on the floor until they were out of sight of the White House and on their way to New York.

VIII

With Luci married off, the press was free to devote their full attention to Lynda Bird. Her romances, rumored and otherwise, kept them busy. At one point, she was dating a White House military aide, but he was replaced by a medical student who in turn was replaced by the movie actor George Hamilton. The relationship seemed to be thriving but there was no sign of an engagement ring.

After graduating from the University of Texas, Lynda Bird took a job as a magazine editor in New York while Hamilton continued to jaunt around the world making movies. They managed to see each other often enough to persuade the press that marriage was a distinct possibility. Then early one morning in 1967, just about a year after Luci's wedding, Lynda Bird slipped into her parents' bedroom to announce that she was going to marry Charles Robb, a marine officer who was the captain of the White House color guard.

George Hamilton, not to mention most of the nation's working press, was totally surprised by the news. And what news it was. Lynda Bird Johnson's marriage—scheduled for four P.M. on Saturday, December 9, 1967—was going to be the first White House wedding in fifty-three years.

Lynda Bird's white silk-satin wedding gown was long-sleeved with a high collar and a front panel outlined in embroidered silk flowers studded with seed pearls. Her attendants wore red velvet. The ceremony was performed on an altar surmounted by a gold cross and decorated with ficus trees and masses of greens dotted with tiny white lights. It was over by 4:16 and Lynda and Chuck marched out of the East Room under an arch of swords held by his brother marine officers in their full dress uniforms.

In contrast to earlier White House weddings, there was no hope of barring the press. As a small concession to family privacy, however, the cameras and lighting equipment were hidden behind poles draped in white to match the walls of the East Room and the networks were allowed to shoot only during the wedding procession and at the beginning of the reception—twenty minutes of footage, all told.

IX

In 1971, President and Mrs. Richard M. Nixon's older daughter, Tricia, became the first, but surely not the last, White House bride to be married in the Rose Garden. Until a few weeks before her engagement was announced, the gossip columnists had failed to notice that Tricia was being seen more and more in the company of a young Harvard Law student from New York City named Edward Cox.

Apparently, the press can only concentrate on one presidential daughter at a time, so for a long while their attention was almost completely focused on Tricia's sister, Julie, who had married Dwight David Eisenhower II, the only grandson of President Eisenhower, about a month before her father was sworn in as president. Julie and David had met some eighteen years earlier when Richard Nixon served as Eisenhower's vice president. There were dozens of photos of the two of them together as children, not to mention their families' political prominence, so from the media's point of view, it was a marriage made in heaven.

I'm sure Tricia was more than happy to have her sister be the center of attention since it gave her a chance to conduct her own romance in private. She and her future husband had known each other since 1964 when Richard Nixon joined a New York law firm after his 1960 defeat for the presidency. They met at a school dance but the relationship took off after Cox, then a Princeton freshman, served as Tricia's escort at the International Debutant Ball.

Marriage was out of the question because the young people were still in school, but by the time Cox was in his second year of law school, it was a different story. By then, the press had finally begun to notice that Edward Cox was spending a significant number of holidays at the White House and Camp David. For several weeks, rumors were rampant. They were finally confirmed on March 17, 1971, when President Nixon announced Tricia's engagement at a St. Patrick's Day reception at the White House.

The wedding was set for four P.M. on Saturday, June 12. Outdoor weddings are always a gamble, even in the normally sunny month of June. Everything was set for a Rose Garden ceremony, but in case of rain, the plans called for moving it to the East Room. I hate to imagine the tension in the family quarters as the weather reports came in. The forecast indicated a fifty percent chance of showers, and as predicted, it began to drizzle about an hour before the ceremony.

President Nixon strolled down to the press tent that had been set up on the South Lawn and informed the reporters that the Nixons had advised their daughter to play it safe and move indoors. Tricia had refused. "I want a Rose Garden wedding," she insisted.

According to the meteorologists, who must have been

dreading the president's wrath if they got it wrong, the rain would not last very long. Based on that information, the ceremony was postponed to 4:30. Miraculously, the rain stopped and the wedding began. Tricia and Ed had barely become Mr. and Mrs. Cox when the rain resumed. Everyone fled indoors where there were plenty of refreshments including three kinds of champagne, all domestic.

In addition to the weather, Tricia's wedding produced two other causes for anxiety. Her father was so nervous about dancing in public that he asked the press corps to send in some sympathetic reporters—"people who know nothing about dancing"—when it was time for the obligatory dances. Although he looked nervous, the president performed no worse than any other father of the bride.

The second source of anxiety was the 355-pound, seven-foot-high wedding cake. The recipe had been published in advance and several well-known food writers had tried to duplicate it without success. One attempt resulted in something that looked and tasted like baked sludge. The actual product proved to be edible as well as beautiful.

Around seven o'clock, the couple, still in their wedding clothes, departed to the music of a small combo playing "Toot, Toot, Tootsie, Good-bye." Unlike previous White House newlyweds, there was no attempt at a stealthy exit. Their black limousine was parked at the North Portico and their destination was later revealed to be a private hideaway with security provided by the Secret Service—Camp David.

X

There is no question that White House weddings are special. The setting is unique and the White House staff are experts at providing the very best in food, music, flowers, and gracious service. A White House bride is not only a star on her wedding day, she can claim a place in the history of the nation's most famous house.

Do I regret not having been married at 1600 Pennsylvania Avenue? Not in the least. I wasn't ready to get married when Dad was in the White House. For one thing, I was determined to have a career as a concert singer. For another, even more important, I hadn't met the right man. When I finally achieved both those goals, I was more than happy to be far away from Washington. My wedding took place at Trinity Episcopal Church in Independence, Missouri, where my parents had been married in 1919. The reception, too, was the same place theirs had been—219 North Delaware Street, my mother's, and later my own, childhood home. It suited me just fine.

Questions for Discussion

1. What are the advantages of getting married in the White House?

2. Are there any drawbacks to having a White House wedding?

3. Should the media be allowed to cover the event?

There have been more dogs than presidents in the White House, but Fala, pictured here with his master, is without question the most famous. Credit: Franklin D. Roosevelt Library

Talking Dogs and Other Unnatural Curiosities

PRESIDENT JOHN F. KENNEDY'S press secretary, Pierre Salinger, was awakened one morning at three A.M. by a call from White House reporter Helen Thomas.

"I wouldn't call you at an ungodly hour like this, Pierre, if it weren't important," she said. "But we have a report that one of Caroline's hamsters has died. Would you check it out for me?"

The hamster was indeed dead—drowned in the president's bathtub—but the story wouldn't have merited even a single line in the press if the rodent hadn't succumbed in the White House.

White House pets are, and always have been, big news. Algonquin, the calico pony that belonged to Theodore Roosevelt's son Archie, was constantly being written up in the papers. Warren G. Harding's Airedale, Laddie Boy, had his picture taken almost as often as his master. When Lyndon Johnson mistreated one of his beagles by picking him up by the ears, the story made headlines around the world.

In most cases, presidents don't mind being upstaged by their pets. If they did, you can be sure the creatures would be out of sight when the press showed up. John F. Kennedy gave orders for the White House kennel keeper to have one or two of the family dogs rush to greet him whenever he returned from a trip. Maybe it was a publicity stunt. Maybe he really missed them. Whatever the explanation, it provided great photo ops.

JFK was not the first president to note that a pet can do wonders for a politician's image. When Herbert Hoover was running for president in 1928, one of his campaign managers circulated a picture of Hoover smiling warmly as he held the front paws of his German shepherd, King Tut. The picture helped dispel Hoover's dour image and made him look more like the compassionate man he truly was.

A pet can also come in handy when a president wants to divert attention from sticky issues. Franklin D. Roosevelt, who hated personal confrontations, often used his Scottish terrier, Fala, to avoid them. Once, when FDR had an appointment with a government official who was planning to tell him something he didn't want to hear, the president made sure that Fala was ushered into the Oval Office at the same time.

Before the man could get down to business, FDR took a ball from his desk drawer and began showing him some of Fala's tricks. Then Fala had an accident on the rug and by the time the puddle was mopped up, the president's next appointment was announced. The man left without ever getting a chance to speak his piece.

II

Dogs are not the only pets that have lived in the White House, but somehow they always get the most press coverage. Perhaps it's because they're more photogenic than the competition, which has included goats, birds, snakes, lizards, rats, and raccoons. I also think dogs have a talent for getting attention.

I'll never forget my one and only dog, an Irish setter puppy named Mike, that was given to me by one of my father's cabinet members not long after we moved into the White House. Talk about getting attention! One of Mike's favorite habits was bounding into my lap whenever I sat down. I simply could not convince him that long and lanky Irish setters were not cut out to be lapdogs.

Mike once leaped into a pool in the White House garden and my mother's secretary jumped in to rescue him. Knowing very little about dogs, she didn't realize that setters are good swimmers. She emerged from the pool dripping wet and hopping mad. Mike, of course, loved every minute of it.

Mike was a model of good behavior compared to some of the dogs that have lived in the White House. Dwight Eisenhower's Weimaraner, Heidi, left endless stains on the White House rugs and also had a bad habit of leaping up in front of Mamie whenever a photographer tried to take her picture.

I don't know what crimes Ulysses S. Grant's son Jesse's dogs committed, but several of them died suddenly and under mysterious circumstances. I suspect they were executed for some malfeasance by a member of the White House staff. President Grant thought so, too. After several unsuccessful attempts at dog-owning, Jesse was presented with a fine Newfoundland. His father promptly called the White House steward into his office. Without mentioning the string of unexplained deaths, Grant said, "Jesse has a new dog. You may have noticed that his former pets have been peculiarly unfortunate. When this dog dies, every employee in the White House will at once be discharged."

The dog, Faithful, lived to a ripe old age.

III

Many presidential families already owned pets that they brought with them when they moved to the White House. But no matter how many pets they had, people inevitably gave them a few more.

When President Kennedy attended a summit meeting in Vienna with Russian premier Nikita Khrushchev, it was not a particularly cordial encounter. But Khrushchev was charmed by Jacqueline Kennedy and later sent her a large collection of gifts, including a fluffy white mongrel named Pushinka for Caroline. Despite her questionable bloodlines, Pushinka had an illustrious background. She was the daughter of Strelka, the dog the Russians had sent on one of their early space missions.

At that time, the United States and the Soviet Union were in the midst of the Cold War, so the Secret Service was understandably suspicious of Pushinka. For all anyone knew, she might have an electronic bug implanted in her tail. Before the dog could be admitted to the White House, she had to undergo a security check. Fortunately, she turned out to be clean.

In 1855, Commodore Matthew C. Perry returned from his historic voyage to Japan, a trip that opened that country to trade with the West. Perry brought back several crates full of gifts for President Franklin Pierce, including Japanese silks, porcelains, and fans. The gift that appealed to the president most was a collection of seven tiny canines that were known in Asia as "sleeve dogs."

Pierce kept one of the dogs at the White House. The others were given to friends, including Secretary of War Jefferson Davis, who was so delighted with the creature that he carried him around in his pocket.

Most probably the dogs were Japanese spaniels or chin chins, now known as Japanese chins. They lived in the Imperial Palace and were often given to important foreign visitors. The name "sleeve dog" comes from the fact that they could be carried in the sleeve of a kimono.

IV

There have been quite a few cats in the White House, but most of them have kept a low profile. Cats are much too cool to curry favor with the press. They are also experts at hiding under beds or curling up in closets to avoid being interviewed. But if they want attention, they know exactly how to get it.

Theodore Roosevelt's family had two cats, Slippers and Tom Quartz. Slippers had a habit of wandering off but the White House staff noticed that he invariably reappeared when an important dinner was scheduled. The dinners always included a fish course and he was probably thinking of the leftovers.

Calvin Coolidge's pet collection included a pair of cats named Tiger and Blacky. Tiger was an alley cat who came wandering in from Pennsylvania Avenue one day and decided to stay. Blacky, whose ancestry was equally undistinguished, was sent to the president by a nurse in Massachusetts because she didn't have room for him.

Blacky was a hunter and was such a menace to the squirrels, birds, and rabbits that inhabit the President's Park that he had to be kept in the guardhouse by the front gate in the spring and summer when the wildlife was out in force.

When he was not playing serial killer on the South Lawn, Blacky's favorite pastime was riding in the White House elevator. He would sit and wait for someone to open the door for him, then he would hop onto the seat and ride up and down for hours, obviously gathering his strength for another run at the wildlife.

When nine-year-old Amy Carter moved into the White House in 1977, she brought along her Siamese cat, Misty Malarky Ying Yang. The cat seemed to know her place. Aside from posing for a few photos, she tended to shun the limelight, but as it turned out, she was simply waiting for the right moment to dazzle the public with her charms.

The moment came when Amy's parents, Rosalynn and Jimmy Carter, held their first state dinner for President and Mrs. José López-Portillo of Mexico. The Carters welcomed the López-Portillos at the North Portico and escorted them to the second floor for a private visit. After half an hour or so, it was time to go downstairs and greet the other guests.

With the Color Team preceding them, the Marine Band playing, and their guests waiting expectantly at the bottom of the Grand Staircase, the Carters looked down and saw that

Misty Malarky had appeared from nowhere and was padding down the stairs in front of them.

The next White House cat of note was Socks Clinton, who arrived in 1993. Socks is a real rags to riches story. The Clintons picked him up as a stray in Arkansas and gave him a home in the Governor's Mansion in Little Rock. A few years later, he had taken another leap forward and was living in the White House.

For the first few years, it was a dream existence. Socks whiled away his days napping in the sunshine on the South Lawn or poking through the papers on the president's secretary's desk. He also became an instant celebrity and was inundated with fan letters, all of which he dutifully answered, signing his responses with a paw print.

Then in 1997, Socks's carefree life was disrupted. The Clintons adopted a chocolate Labrador retriever named Buddy. Not only did Socks drop to second place in the White House pet standings, but he had to put up with all sorts of barking and growling from his replacement.

Cat and dog fights can be contained in the White House, where there's plenty of room and more than enough help to keep them from getting out of hand. But the Clintons knew it would be impossible to deal with the situation after they left 1600 Pennsylvania Avenue. They decided to take Buddy with them and give Socks to Clinton's secretary, Betty Currie, whose White House desk had long been one of his favorite haunts.

The latest White House cat in residence, Willie, has been a member of the Bush family for over ten years, but she has never tried to capitalize on the relationship. On the contrary, she keeps such a low profile that most people don't even know she exists, which doesn't bother Willie in the slightest. Willie spends most of her time hiding from her owners, napping under one of their beds, or munching on tuna-flavored kitty treats.

V

During the Kennedy administration there were always at least a dozen exotic pets in residence, including lambs, guinea pigs, hamsters, birds, and rabbits. Among the pets in the Kennedys' private menagerie was Caroline Kennedy's pony, Macaroni, who divided his time between his stable at the White House and the Kennedy home in Virginia. When he was in Washington, he roamed freely around the White House grounds. One day Macaroni wandered over to the West Wing and stood staring into one of the tall windows in the Oval Office. President Kennedy stared back. After a few minutes, he went over, opened the door, and motioned to Macaroni to come in. The pony thought about it for a few minutes, then turned around and ambled off.

Macaroni missed his chance to become the first pony in history to visit the Oval Office. He may have considered this only a minor accomplishment in view of the fact that another pony had gotten as far as the second-floor living quarters.

When nine-year-old Archie Roosevelt was stricken with both measles and whooping cough, his younger brother, Quentin, decided that a visit from his pony, Algonquin, would cheer him up. Quentin persuaded one of the White House footmen to help him coax the 350-pound animal into the White House elevator. Algonquin was jittery about the venture until he became absorbed in studying himself in the elevator mirror and gave the footman a chance to press the button. The invalid was so happy to see Algonquin trotting into his bedroom that he immediately began to recover.

Abraham and Mary Lincoln's two younger sons, Willie and Tad, had their own ponies, which they rode around the grounds under the watchful eye of a White House messenger. When Willie died of typhoid fever, Tad lost all interest in his pony. The animal was replaced in his affections by a pair of goats. Strange as it may seem today, goats were popular pets in the nineteenth and early twentieth centuries. They were known for being gentle and good-natured and they could be hitched to small carts to give children a safe ride.

When they weren't busy pulling Tad around in his cart, Nanny and Nanko made a beeline for the White House flower beds, destroying the plants and driving the gardener into a frenzy. The only solution was to keep them in the stables. Nanko was the better behaved of the pair and when he was put in the stables, he stayed there. Nanny, however, always managed to get out and, of course, headed straight for the garden.

To keep the goat from causing too much destruction, the president had her brought into the White House, but instead of staying docilely in the basement, she wandered upstairs and curled up on Tad's bed. The housekeeper shooed her outside where she attacked the flower beds once again. That was her last foray. The next day Nanny disappeared. Somehow I don't think it was a coincidence.

Among the other White House children who had goats to pull them around were President Rutherford B. Hayes's youngest son, Scott, and Benjamin Harrison's grandson, Ben Mc-

Kee. Ben's goat, His Whiskers, could often be seen on the front lawn of the White House with the little boy in tow.

One day, as President Harrison was standing on the North Portico, about to leave for an appointment, His Whiskers abruptly shifted into high gear and went tearing down Pennsylvania Avenue with Ben and his cart bouncing along behind him. The president, in his frock coat and high silk hat, took off after them, waving his cane and calling for His Whiskers to stop.

The goat finally slowed down and Harrison was able to grab him by his harness. Instead of finding his grandson screaming in fright, as the president had expected, Ben was fine. He told his grandfather that the ride had been great fun.

VI

Among the various animals that were sent to the White House during the Coolidge administration was a raccoon. It was intended to be the main course at Thanksgiving dinner, but Coolidge, a traditionalist, decided to stick with turkey. He took a liking to the raccoon and decided to keep her as a pet. He christened her Rebecca, installed her in a pen near the Oval Office, and gave her a steady diet of her favorite foods, shrimp and persimmons.

When Coolidge let Rebecca out of her pen, she would follow him around the White House, causing quite a stir among visitors, who thought there was a wild animal loose on the premises. They weren't entirely mistaken. Rebecca could be pretty wild when she wanted to be. Since raccoons have forepaws shaped like tiny hands, they are amazingly dexterous and can get into all sorts of mischief. Rebecca could unscrew lightbulbs, open cabinet doors, and unpot palms.

Being a nocturnal animal, Rebecca was at her best after dark. On pleasant evenings, she and the president used to take long walks together. It must have been quite a sight to see Coolidge strolling along with Rebecca on her leash waddling beside him.

Theodore Roosevelt's children shared their father's love of wild creatures. As a boy in New York, Teddy once met a friend of his mother's on a streetcar. As he tipped his hat politely, several frogs jumped out and landed in the woman's lap.

During their years in the White House, the young Roosevelts had an assortment of exotic pets including a parrot named Loretta, a blue macaw named Eli Yale, and a badger named Josiah.

Whatever you think of badgers, you'll probably agree that they are infinitely more appealing than snakes. The Roosevelt children had those, too. Quentin, the youngest of the Roosevelt sons, once went barreling into the Oval Office to show his father a pair of snakes he had found in the garden. The president, who was conferring with some of his cabinet members, directed him to wait outside.

Quentin retreated to the reception room and promptly struck up a conversation with a group of congressmen who had come to call on the president. The men displayed a great interest in the snakes until it dawned on them that they were real. By then, it was too late to retreat. When the president emerged from his meeting some minutes later, he found one of the congressmen gingerly helping Quentin retrieve a snake that had slithered up the man's coat sleeve.

The best known of the White House snakes (nonhuman

variety) belonged to Roosevelt's teenaged daughter, Alice. She called it Emily Spinach "because it was as green as spinach and as thin as my aunt Emily." Aunt Emily was her stepmother Edith Roosevelt's sister, Emily Carow.

According to Alice, the snake was affectionate and completely harmless, but the press made such a fuss about it that, as Alice said later, "one would have thought that I was harboring a boa constrictor in the White House."

Unfortunately, Emily Spinach met an untimely end. Alice came home one day and found it dead in its box. Worse yet, it was lying in such an unnatural position that she had no doubt it had been killed. Alice was furious and would have found some way to exact revenge on the murderer, if only she had known who it was.

VII

Not all the animals that lived at the White House were kept as pets. In preautomobile days, there was always a stable full of horses, some for riding, others to pull presidential carriages. Andrew Jackson and Ulysses S. Grant also kept racehorses and Zachary Taylor brought along Old Whitey, the horse he had ridden during the Mexican War, although the poor steed was so ancient that he was good for very little except grazing on the White House lawn.

The only thing that could distract Old Whitey from his grazing was parade music. Every time he heard a brass band he would go looking for his place in the line of march. When the Marine Band appeared on the South Lawn for their evening concerts, Old Whitey had to be sequestered in the stables.

Otherwise, he would have been breathing down the musicians' necks trying to find out when the parade was going to start.

I can understand horses at the White House, even Old Whitey, but cows? I have to keep reminding myself that keeping livestock in the backyard wasn't so strange in the nineteenth century. In those days, there weren't any supermarkets or convenience stores where you could pick up a quart of milk whenever you needed it.

The cows used to graze in an area just beyond the south fence (now the Ellipse), but they were locked up at night because for many years cattle rustling was a serious problem in Washington. The cows were milked by a cowman and the milk was stored in crocks for use in the White House kitchen.

The last cow to graze on the White House lawn was Pauline Wayne. She was sent to another pasture during President William Howard Taft's administration when commercial dairies became common and milk no longer had to be obtained directly from its source.

VIII

Other animals come and go but none of them have been able to edge dogs out of the White House spotlight. Almost every president has had at least one. Herbert Hoover had eight in addition to the famous King Tut. They ranged from a small black poodle called Tar Baby to a giant wolfhound named Shamrock.

Calvin Coolidge had almost as many dogs as Herbert Hoover. They included two chows named Timmy and Blackberry, and a pair of pure white collies named Prudence Prim and Rob Roy. Rob Roy was far and away the president's favorite, and the collie made sure everyone knew it. He accompanied Coolidge to his office every morning, walking directly in front of him looking neither to the left nor the right in a canine imitation of the Presidential Color Team.

Rob Roy's greatest claim to fame was having his portrait painted with Mrs. Coolidge. In the picture he's looking up at her with what I used to think was adoration on his face. I've since learned that she got him to pose by feeding him candy during the sittings. He may just be looking for another handout.

The portrait, by Howard Chandler Christy, hangs in the White House and has probably produced an acute case of jealousy in every other first dog who has seen it. I must say it's a remarkable painting not only because Mrs. Coolidge is so attractive, but because of the striking color scheme. The artist painted her wearing a bright red dress, which stands in vivid contrast to the snow-white dog at her side.

Calvin Coolidge had wanted his wife to wear a white brocaded satin gown that was one of his favorites, but Howard Chandler Christy objected. He felt that the combination of the red dress and the white dog would make a more pleasing picture.

The president deferred to the artist's judgment but not before offering one last argument: "She could still wear the dress and we'd dye the dog."

IX

Traphes Bryant, who was the White House kennel keeper during the Kennedy, Johnson, and Nixon administrations, rated Lyndon Johnson as the greatest pet lover of all our presidents. When the Johnsons moved into the White House, they brought along a pair of beagle puppies that had been given to their younger daughter, Luci. Their names were Him and Her and they were soon joined by another gift dog, a white collie named Blanco.

Lyndon often took time out from his busy schedule to play with the dogs and when he stepped out of his office and gave a whistle, they would come bounding over to him, each trying to be the first to get a pat on the head.

Her died when she was a little over a year old after swallowing a small rock she found on the White House lawn. A couple of years later, Him followed Her to the grave. He was indulging in his favorite sport, chasing squirrels, when he was hit by a White House car.

LBJ was heartbroken. He was not consoled by the fact that Blanco remained. Although Blanco was a fine-looking dog, he had very little to offer in the way of brains or personality. Then Yuki appeared.

Luci and her husband, Patrick Nugent, found him at a gas station in Austin, Texas. Nobody knew whom he belonged to so they took him home and when he and LBJ met, it was love at first sight. Yuki went back to Washington with the president and had the run of the White House. He hung out in the Oval Office, sat under the table at cabinet meetings, and was introduced to statesmen and celebrities. Yuki flew back to Texas with the Johnsons on Air Force One when LBJ's term was over.

What made Lyndon Johnson, whose dogs had always had impeccable pedigrees, become so attached to a homeless mutt? According to LBJ, there were two reasons: First, "He speaks with a Texas accent," and second, but even more important, "He likes me."

I've often thought how fitting it was that when Lyndon Johnson died suddenly of a heart attack in 1973, he was alone, except for Yuki.

X

Warren Harding's dog, Laddie Boy, once gave an interview to the Washington *Star*, but since then dogs have gotten even smarter. In 1990, President George H. W. Bush's English springer spaniel, Mildred Kerr Bush, actually wrote a book. She freely admitted that she didn't do it entirely on her own; she dictated it to First Lady Barbara Bush. The book became a best-seller and raised almost a million dollars for the Barbara Bush Foundation for Family Literacy.

Millie was very much in the news during the Bush administration, particularly after she gave birth to six puppies at the White House in 1989. The Bushes got so many letters welcoming her brood that they had a thank-you card made up with their signatures and Millie and her offsprings' paw prints.

One of Millie's puppies went to George and Barbara Bush's granddaughters, Jenna and Barbara, in Texas. The girls named her Spot Fletcher after one of their heroes, Scott Fletcher, who played baseball for the Texas Rangers. When Fletcher was traded to another team, they dropped the dog's last name and now she is known simply as Spot.

In 2001, Spot followed in her mother's footsteps by moving into the White House, giving her the distinction of being the only second-generation presidential pet in White House history, and enabling her to feel quite superior to the first family's other dog, a Scottish terrier puppy named Barney.

XI

Speaking of Scottish terriers, no discussion of White House pets would be complete without some observations on the most famous one of all: Franklin D. Roosevelt's Scottie, Fala. He was not the first of FDR's dogs. There were several others before him but they all faded into the background when Fala came along in the spring of 1940.

Fala and the president became all but inseparable. The Scottie would sleep on a blanket in Roosevelt's bedroom and play on the grass outside the Oval Office. When the president went for a car ride, Fala was usually perched beside him on the seat. The Secret Service gave him the code name "The Informer," because when Roosevelt traveled by train, the dog had to be walked, alerting everyone to the fact that the president was on board.

Fala was at home in the White House, in FDR's home at Hyde Park, and in Warm Springs, Georgia, where Roosevelt went to be treated for the polio that had paralyzed his legs in 1921. When FDR and Prime Minister Winston Churchill of Great Britain met on a British battleship off the coast of Newfoundland in the summer of 1941, Fala went along and had his photograph taken with the two world leaders.

Fala was with Roosevelt in Warm Springs, Georgia, when the president was stricken with, and died almost instantly from, a cerebral hemorrhage. The dog returned to the White House with the body of his master and was eventually taken to live with Eleanor Roosevelt. He died in the spring of 1952 and lies buried beside Franklin D. Roosevelt in the Hyde Park Rose Garden. He has also been immortalized in bronze at the Franklin D. Roosevelt Memorial in Washington, where he can be seen sitting at Roosevelt's feet just as he did in life.

Questions for Discussion

1. How can a pet be an asset to a president?

2. Can you think of some reasons why goats and raccoons might not make good pets?

3. Why are dogs the most popular White House pets?

Here is a shot of President Ronald Reagan talking to reporters in the Oval Office. Their relationship appears to be a whole lot warmer than it really was. Credit: Courtesy Ronald Reagan Library

☆ 13 ☆

Minding the Media

THERE'S ONE SECTION of the North Lawn of the White House that is covered with gravel rather than grass. This particular part of the President's Park, which is known to insiders as Pebble Beach, is the place where television reporters stand when they're delivering the latest news from the Oval Office. TV watchers never see the gravel, but they get a fine view of the North Portico of the White House and, although it probably never occurs to them, a chance to observe freedom of the press in action.

The Founding Fathers included freedom of the press in the Bill of Rights because they believed that an informed citizenry was essential to the survival of a democracy. As James Madison, one of those founders, noted, "A popular government without popular information or the means of acquiring it is but a prologue to a farce or a tragedy, or perhaps both."

I'm quite sure no president of the United States would disagree with James Madison or with the Bill of Rights he helped to frame. In principle, every chief executive believes in the

First Amendment guarantee of a free press. In practice, however, almost all of them have been wary of, if not downright hostile to, the men and women who represent it.

II

The war between the presidents and the press has been going on ever since the country began. President George Washington accused the journalists of his era of abusing him as if he were a "common pickpocket." John Adams was certain the tribe of "scribblers" had deprived him of a second term.

To outwit his enemies in the press, Thomas Jefferson made one Washington newspaper, the *National Intelligencer,* the unofficial White House organ. Its editors frequently dined with the president, then rushed back to the printing presses to peddle the latest party line.

Andrew Jackson went Jefferson one better. He not only brought Kentuckian Francis Preston Blair to Washington to found the *Globe,* he made him a member of his "kitchen cabinet," the group of unofficial advisers who met with the president at all hours of the night.

Francis Preston Blair gave his name to Blair House, which he purchased around 1830, giving him easy access to his patron and prime source of news. Needless to say, the *Globe's* loyalty to Jackson was total. When a cholera epidemic ravaged Washington, D.C., the *Globe* barely mentioned it. Blair was too busy filling his columns with pro-Jackson stories and endorsements.

III

Women were practically nonexistent in this dawn of White House journalism. For years I nurtured an admiration for one of the pioneers, a feisty female named Anne Royall, who published a newspaper called *Paul Pry* that was a forerunner of today's supermarket tabloids. (She lifted the title from a hit London comedy about a character who specialized in sticking his nose into other people's business.) Not a little of my admiration for Anne was based on the story that in the late 1820s she caught that ultimate presidential sourpuss, John Quincy Adams, swimming in the Potomac without a stitch on (something he did regularly). Anne supposedly sat on his clothes and refused to depart until he gave her an interview. Unfortunately, in the course of researching this book, I concluded the story (sigh) is not true.

Anne Royall nevertheless deserves a salute for her perseverance. Although her paper's circulation was never very high, she was a fixture on the Washington scene for forty years.

IV

By the time Anne Royall retired, things had begun happening in the newspaper world that made insider journalism passé. Steam-driven presses replaced the laborious hand-presses on which apprentices broke their backs, turning out one or two sheets at a time. Soon a journalist named James Gordon Bennett decided he could sell papers for as little as a penny a copy and still make money. That startling idea led

Bennett to conclude he did not need a president's favor, or the backing of his enemies, to prosper. The era of the president as fair game for any and all reporters dawned.

Bennett became the owner and editor of the hugely successful New York *Herald* and a man almost as famous as the president, whoever he happened to be. His style of no-holds-barred reporting found one of its first targets in Martin Van Buren. According to Bennett: "Martin Van Buren and his atrocious associates form one of the original causes of the terrible moral, political and commercial desolation that spreads over the country."

The *Herald's* abuse opened the door for similar attacks on succeeding presidents. James Polk, for instance, was called "Jim Thumb," an uncomplimentary comparison to Tom Thumb, P. T. Barnum's famous midget.

Almost as startling as this casual abuse by the press is the access these scribes had to the president. One reporter described how he strolled into the White House "unheralded" and thrust himself into a reception President Pierce was giving for "a bevy of ladies." The president greeted him "politely" and even introduced him to Mrs. Pierce. That did not stop the news hawk from launching into a diatribe against his host in the very next sentence.

V

In the crisis of the Civil War, the press acquired even more power. Thanks to the country's hunger for news, newspaper circulation soared and, with the invention of the telegraph and the rise of the railroads, stories could be quickly disseminated throughout the country.

That realistic man, Abraham Lincoln, saw newspapers as crucial to maintaining public support for the war. Lincoln seldom, if ever, turned away a reporter's request for information.

By the time the Civil War ended, newspapers had become so popular that succeeding presidents regarded them the way kings in the Middle Ages viewed dukes and barons—potential rivals for power, to be propitiated or outwitted or defied, depending on the circumstances. No less than 150 reporters were now permanently based in Washington, D.C., sending back news to their home papers.

Andrew Johnson, Lincoln's harried successor, gave long interviews to individual reporters, which did not save him from impeachment, though it may have rescued him from conviction. Ulysses Grant decided to tell reporters as little as possible. His wife, Julia, filled the gap and became the first presidential spouse to be interviewed by the press. When President James Garfield was shot in 1881, reporters were allowed to set up a press office on the second floor of the White House and transmit their stories from the telegraph room.

The steadily increasing power of the press was one of several reasons why Grover Cleveland appointed a former newspaper editor, Daniel Lamont, as his secretary. Lamont performed many of the duties that would later be taken over by the White House press secretary. Essentially he served as a buffer between the president and reporters, whom Cleveland lumped into a single epithet: "the dirty gang."

VI

Grover Cleveland must have been appalled when a reporter appeared, quite literally, on his doorstep in 1896. William Price had come to the capital from a small town in South Carolina hoping to get a job on the *Washington Evening Star*. Looking for a way to get rid of him, the city editor sent him to the White House with orders to come back with a story. If he got one, the job was his.

As the editor well knew, the chances of getting any news from the Cleveland White House were almost nil. But Price was unfazed by the challenge. As the editor of a small-town weekly, he had gotten his news by hanging around the local train station and interviewing the people who arrived each day. Deciding to use the same strategy at the White House, he stood outside the North Portico and talked to the visitors who went in and out. "Fatty" Price—he weighed three hundred pounds—soon had a job at the *Evening Star*.

With the outbreak of the Spanish-American War in the spring of 1898, the press finally managed to win working space in the White House. President William McKinley agreed to let Price and other reporters gather in the east hall on the second floor. There they could write their stories, interview visitors going in and out of the president's office, and badger his secretary for scraps of news.

Theodore Roosevelt ordered Charles McKim to include a pressroom in the new executive office building—today's West Wing. The scribes were even provided with telephones, eliminating the need for them to send their copy to Western Union by bicycle. There was something in all this for the president, of course. The press was instantly accessible anytime he wanted to barrage an opponent with hostile headlines.

VII

With Teddy Roosevelt, the country got a president who showed future Oval Office occupants how to handle the press and set the style for making the White House the red-hot center of the nation's politics. We have often heard about the way Theodore Roosevelt turned the presidency into a "bully pulpit," but not many people realize how much manipulation of news and newsmen this involved.

Teddy (he hated the name) produced a gallery of presidential tricks still in use today. Bad news was released at the end of the day on Friday because many people slept late on Saturday and skipped reading the papers. Middling news was released in time for the Sunday papers, when hard up editors were likely to put it on the front page for lack of anything more interesting. TR was also the master of the trial balloon, an idea or proposal that he floated through some willing reporter and then might deny or even denounce if the public disliked it.

VIII

Woodrow Wilson's opinion of the press was on a par with Grover Cleveland's. "Those contemptible spies, the newspapermen," he called them on one occasion. Nevertheless, Wilson became the first chief executive to hold regularly scheduled press conferences. Unfortunately, they were not very successful. The president, with his college professor background, lectured the reporters as if they were not-too-bright freshmen, and when their stories failed to get passing grades, he stopped seeing them almost entirely.

Although Wilson considered his press conferences a waste of time—and the reporters were inclined to agree with him—the fact that they had been established was an important step in the relationship between the White House and the press. The relationship was further formalized in 1914 when the newsmen organized the White House Correspondents Association. The move led to stricter rules about who could, and could not, attend presidential press conferences and created a forum where complaints by and against reporters could be heard.

IX

Although you would never guess it from all the stories about his taciturnity, Calvin Coolidge supplied more wordage to the press during his tenure than Theodore Roosevelt and Woodrow Wilson combined. He was not only the first president to make radio addresses, he made them at the rate of one a month. He also met with the press twice a week.

Coolidge followed the presidential custom of accepting only written questions submitted to him in advance. That precedent was broken by Franklin D. Roosevelt, who let the reporters fire away. FDR also revived regular press conferences, which had all but disappeared during the Hoover administration. Roosevelt turned them into a Washington institution.

Once or twice a week, FDR would invite about twenty newspaper and radio reporters into the Oval Office and let them pelt him with questions that he sometimes answered and more often ducked, dodged, or joked away with his marvelous combination of charm and wit.

FDR's amicable relations with the press did not last. Some journalists grew disillusioned when he failed to cure the Great Depression. Others became skeptical after the outbreak of World War II when he barred them from covering such major stories as his 1941 meeting with Winston Churchill at Placentia Bay, Newfoundland, and the 1943 Teheran conference with Churchill and Joseph Stalin. In both instances, British reporters broke the stories.

X

Meanwhile, First Lady Eleanor Roosevelt was changing White House coverage in a very important way. She started holding press conferences—for women reporters only. The Washington bureau chiefs, male to the last grizzled whisker, were thunderstruck. It meant they might have to let women start writing about something more important than the first lady's taste in china.

Mrs. Roosevelt's conferences were not replays of FDR's free-for-alls. The women reporters all wore hats and gloves—and that dreadful topic, politics, was forbidden. Mrs. R. sat among the women, often knitting while they chatted. Only gradually did the topics change from cooking, interior decorating, and White House entertaining to Mrs. Roosevelt's concern for the poor and neglected.

Though Eleanor Roosevelt often spoke up on behalf of black Americans, she never managed to reverse her husband's exclusion of black reporters from the White House, in spite of their frequent petitions. The president's press secretary, Steve Early, offered the not very convincing argument that the blacks represented weeklies, and White House correspondents were supposed to be from daily papers.

The blacks, good reporters, discovered that Early was letting in journalists from weekly trade papers and testily asked: How come? In 1944, after twelve frustrating years, black journalists finally joined the throng in the Oval Office.

XI

FDR's death after only eighty-two days of his fourth term catapulted Harry S Truman into the White House. Although he was often taken to task in the press, historians seem to agree his performance was pretty creditable. But he, too, had more than his share of troubles with reporters, beginning with the very fundamental question of where they were going to meet.

The West Wing was already bursting at the seams, and one of Dad's first orders of business was to find a way to enlarge it. Plans were drawn up for an expansion that would provide more office space, a staff cafeteria, a new pressroom, and an auditorium where press conferences could be held. In December 1945, Congress approved an appropriation that would cover the cost of the added space.

But when a sketch of the proposed addition to the West Wing appeared in the newspapers, the public was convinced that the White House itself was going to be changed and no amount of explanation could persuade them otherwise. Always sensitive to the voice of the voters, Congress amended the appropriation bill and the precise amount allotted for enlarging the West Wing disappeared.

Ironically, it was the president perhaps with the strongest antipathy to the media who finally managed to get them decent facilities. Annoyed at the noisy, messy pressroom adjoining the lobby where his visitors entered, Richard Nixon started looking for new space. He found it in the basement of the West Wing, where Franklin D. Roosevelt had installed the swimming pool he used as therapy for his polio-damaged legs. The swimming pool was torn out and the space was reconfigured to accommodate a press center with a briefing room where the White House press secretary could fill reporters in on the latest news from the Oval Office.

Plans are in the works for a new pressroom to be built under the West Wing drive. When—and if—it is completed, the new facility will spell the end of Pebble Beach, but it seems unlikely that its disappearance will provoke an uproar. No one will miss the crush of lights and cameras on the White House lawn, least of all the TV reporters who have to endure all kinds of bad weather in the course of doing their jobs.

XII

Like presidents before him and since, Dad acquired a low opinion of newspapermen during his White House years. Always mindful of history, he dug into the press relations of previous presidents and was comforted to discover he was not alone.

"It seems that every man in the White House was tortured and bedeviled by the so-called free press," he wrote to his sister. "They were lied about, misrepresented and actually libeled, and they have to take it."

With this as background, you can easily imagine why I administered one of the worst shocks of Dad's postpresidential life when I called him from New York to tell him I had fallen in love and was planning to marry a man named Clifton Daniel.

"What does he do for a living?" Dad asked.

"He's a newspaperman."

There was a moment of thunderstruck silence on the Missouri end of the phone. Finally, gamely, Dad said: "Well, if you love him, that's good enough for me."

(P.S. They got along beautifully.)

XIII

In 1954, Dwight Eisenhower became the first president to hold televised news conferences. Ike was coached in advance by actor Robert Montgomery and the telecasts were carefully stage-managed by Ike's press secretary, who reserved the right to edit the tapes before they were released to the public.

Both televised press conferences and stage-managing were raised to high arts by Ike's successor, John F. Kennedy. JFK's first press conference was broadcast live from the East Room, beginning what one weekly newsmagazine called "a new era in political communication."

The president, who was not only young and handsome but had a quick wit and an engaging manner, apparently had no difficulty pulling whatever facts he needed from his agile brain on demand. Not many people knew that his astute press secretary gave him a thorough briefing on the probable questions just as Ike's had done.

When it came to charming the press, Jack was well on his way to outclassing Franklin D. Roosevelt. He had also mastered the Rooseveltian art of manipulation. He leaked stories, planted news, gave exclusives to favored journalists, and played reporters off against each other. Like FDR, he was not above withholding news from the media when it suited his interests. As he remarked to one of his staff members, "Always remember that their interests and ours ultimately conflict."

XIV

The undeclared war between the press and the president saw the media's greatest triumph when a pair of investigative reporters from *The Washington Post* found an anonymous source who filled them in on the doings in the Nixon White House during the Watergate affair. Their stories made front page news and helped to drive Nixon out of office. But while the press was busy congratulating itself on the victory, the White House was gearing up to fight back.

Under Gerald Ford, Richard Nixon's successor, 1600 Pennsylvania Avenue started to become a media powerhouse in its own right. The press office staff was increased to forty-five people, about seven times more than there were in John F. Kennedy's day.

The trend continued under President Jimmy Carter. In 1978, the Carter press office, now called the Office of Media

Liaison, regularly sent out thousands of press releases, audio-tapes, and films to news organizations each month. The output grew even larger under Presidents Reagan, George H. W. Bush, and Clinton. In this blizzard of information and images, press conferences lost much of their importance. In Ronald Reagan's administration, reporters were often reduced to screaming questions at the president as he boarded his helicopter on the White House lawn.

During the Clinton tenure, press conferences were reduced to the vanishing point. The Clinton White House preferred to rely on its own awesome ability to communicate directly to the American people. The Clinton White House beamed programs to public and commercial television stations at the rate of one a day. Meanwhile the White House Web site (www.whitehouse.gov) was bundling transcripts of the president's speeches over the Internet and streaming live interviews with the president, in which fifteen thousand people could fire E-mail questions at the Oval Office. This led one reporter to suggest that the "White House propaganda machine has . . . clearly been winning the battle" for control of public opinion.

I have too much faith in the people who write and edit and broadcast the news to believe that this can ever be the case. When President George W. Bush took office, his press secretary warned the media not to expect him to hold formal press conferences in the East Room, like many of his predecessors. Instead, he would hold them in the White House briefing room, supplement them with informal chats with reporters, and answer a few questions during photo ops.

I was concerned at first. Then I read an interview with my old friend Helen Thomas, who has been covering the White

House since John F. Kennedy took office in 1961. Helen has made more than one president squirm at a press conference.

Was she concerned about Bush's approach? "I don't think it matters when or where the press conference is held," she said, "just so we really get a crack at him."

She went on to point out that press conferences are the only real chance Americans have to question their president. With Helen and her colleagues around, we are unlikely to lose that chance. That means sooner or later at least some of the truth about what's happening in the White House is going to reach the American people, whether the president likes it or not.

Questions for Discussion

1. Why are presidents wary of the media?

2. How can a good press secretary improve a president's relations with the press?

3. Why should presidents meet with reporters on a regular basis?

☆　　☆　　☆

The man on the left of President Calvin Coolidge is Secret Service agent Edmund Starling. Of the five presidents he protected, Coolidge was his favorite.
Credit: U.S. Secret Service

☆ 14 ☆

Keeping Killers and Kooks at Bay

MY PARENTS HAD to move to Blair House while the White House was undergoing its historic foundation-to-roof reconstruction, but the West Wing was perfectly sound so there was no reason why my father couldn't continue to work in the Oval Office. The only question was: How would he get there?

The West Wing is only a few steps across Pennsylvania Avenue, but Jim Rowley, the Secret Service agent in charge of the White House detail, wanted him to go by car. Dad was not too happy about the idea. "Can you imagine being driven across the street?" he said. But he took Jim's advice.

A couple of years later, Dad had reason to be glad the Secret Service was on the job. On November 1, 1950, around two P.M., two armed Puerto Rican nationalists, Oscar Collazo and Griselio Torresola, approached Blair House. My father and mother were upstairs dressing to go to a ceremony at Arlington National Cemetery. I was far away, preparing to give a concert in Portland, Oregon.

The two gunmen planned to assassinate the president on

229

behalf of Puerto Rican independence. Collazo, who had never fired a pistol before in his life, approached from the east, Torresola from the west. They planned to meet on the front steps of Blair House and charge inside together.

The house was guarded by White House policemen in booths at either end of the building. Another policeman, Donald T. Birdzell, was on duty at the front door, which was open to the mild fall weather. Only a lightly latched screen door prevented access from the street.

Collazo mingled with some tourists as he passed the east booth. When he was within three or four feet of the front door, he whipped out his pistol, aimed it at Birdzell, and pulled the trigger. Nothing happened.

If that pistol had gone off, the plot might well have succeeded. With Birdzell dead, Collazo planned to whirl and shoot the guards in the east booth while his partner took care of the men in the west booth. After that the only person between them and the president would have been the Secret Service man stationed at the head of the stairs to the second floor. The assassins might have shot him, too, leaving the president and first lady unprotected.

Hearing the click of Collazo's gun, Birdzell turned to find him pounding on the jammed pistol. It suddenly went off, striking the policeman in the knee. Not wanting to fire with pedestrians in the area, Birdzell stumbled down the steps to the street before drawing his gun. A Secret Service agent who was with the policeman in the east booth opened fire. Meanwhile, Torresola reached the west booth and quickly pumped two bullets into policeman Leslie Coffelt and another slug into Joseph Downs, the other policeman in the booth. Whirling, he took a second shot at Birdzell and another policeman coming out a basement door. As Torresola paused to reload his gun, the dying Coffelt tottered to the doorway of the west booth and put a bullet in his brain. By this time, three shots fired by other policemen and Secret Service agents had hit Collazo. In less than two minutes twenty-seven shots had been fired.

My parents left for the dedication ceremony on schedule. "A president has to expect these things," Dad said. The next day, at a press conference, he told the reporters, "I was never in any danger. The thing I hate about it is what happened to these young men—one of them killed [Coffelt] and two of them [Downs and Birdzell] badly wounded."

II

There are any number of people who gravitate to Washington from all parts of the country to tell the president their troubles, or to give him advice on his troubles—or to do him serious bodily harm. The Secret Service has been trying to keep them at bay for over one hundred years, with varying degrees of success.

If you have any doubts about the need for the Secret Service, consider these statistics. One in every three presidents has been shot at or otherwise attacked. Four have been killed by assassin's bullets. In the past few decades, Gerald Ford survived two blasts of gunfire and Ronald Reagan came within a hairsbreadth of being killed by a seriously disturbed man who thought shooting a president would impress screen star Jodie Foster.

In the beginning, the president had no protectors. Thomas Jefferson included guardhouses in his plans to complete the

White House but no one, including him, implemented the idea. Luckily, Jefferson, Madison, and Monroe escaped unscathed and unthreatened, except for Madison's encounter with those red-coated pyromaniacs in 1814.

John Quincy Adams and Andrew Jackson displayed no interest in employing bodyguards, although Jackson could have used them. On January 30, 1835, he was striding through the rotunda of the Capitol when an assassin stepped out of the crowd and aimed a pistol at his heart from a distance of about three feet. The gun barked but only the cap exploded, not the charge that fired the bullet. Cursing, the would-be killer whipped another pistol from beneath his coat and pulled that trigger. The same thing happened.

The infuriated Jackson bashed his attacker with his cane and seven or eight congressmen piled on top of the man, who shouted that Jackson was preventing him from becoming king of England.

The two guns were taken to an armory where experts tested them. They were in perfect working order and fired bullets the first time someone pulled their triggers. The experts estimated the odds against both guns failing to work were about 1 in 125,000.

If there is any conclusion that can be drawn from this incident, it may be that some presidents lead charmed lives and others are just unlucky.

III

Abraham Lincoln began receiving death threats almost from the day he was elected. He had won with only forty percent of the popular vote, which left a lot of the country angry. By the time the new president set out for Washington, D.C., in February 1861, most of the South had seceded and the atmosphere was even more rancid. Lincoln's former law partner and a professional detective made the journey with him, armed with knives and pistols.

As the war between the North and the South escalated, so did Lincoln's death threats. There were more than enough to make him acutely conscious of his safety. He saw to it that the doormen and many of the inside servants were armed. A contingent of plainclothesmen from the Washington, D.C., Metropolitan Police was hired with instructions to conceal their guns by wearing suits that were a size too big for them.

In this tense atmosphere, First Lady Mary Lincoln became the victim of an apparent assassination attempt. In July of 1863, she was staying in a house at the Soldiers' Home in northeast Washington, where the Lincolns spent their summers. Confederate and Union armies were locked in a death struggle near the town of Gettysburg, Pennsylvania. Desperate to hear some news, the first lady climbed into her carriage and ordered the driver to head for the White House at top speed.

As they hurtled down the road, the carriage suddenly disintegrated. Mrs. Lincoln and the coachman were flung headfirst into the dirt. By a miracle, they both escaped serious injury. Many people concluded that the carriage had been tampered with in the hope of killing the president.

Another time, when Lincoln was riding out to spend the night at the Soldiers' Home, a gunshot startled his horse. The president thought it was an accidental discharge, until someone inspected his hat and found a bullet hole. Thereafter, he never rode anywhere without a cavalry escort.

Despite his precautions, Lincoln still fell victim to an assassin's bullet. He died because he and his guards wrongly assumed that with the surrender of Robert E. Lee at Appomattox, the Civil War was over and there was no longer any need for vigilance. The moral of the tragic story of Lincoln's decision to go to Ford's Theater on Good Friday night is one that the modern Secret Service never forgets. A president is never safe, anytime, anywhere.

IV

En route to that grim conclusion, two other presidents had extremely narrow escapes. Lincoln's successor, Andrew Johnson, stepped out of his office on the second floor one day to find a madman with a loaded gun rampaging down the hall. Johnson shouted for help and several servants and aides leaped on the man, who for some unknown reason did not pull the trigger.

Next on the close call list was Benjamin Harrison. One evening in 1891, shouts and the sounds of a struggle drew him to the Red Room. He found two doorkeepers wrestling with a deranged man wielding a knife. The president helped the doormen pin the intruder down and cut a length of window cord to tie him up.

These incidents were quickly forgotten, but the deaths of two other presidents could not be so easily overlooked. James Garfield was struck down by the bullets of a crazed job seeker as he walked through the Baltimore & Potomac Railroad Station in July of 1881. Next to die was William McKinley, in a scene that no modern Secret Service man can read about without wincing.

The president was in Buffalo, New York, to open an exposition. On September 5, 1901, he arrived at the exposition grounds for a public reception that was supposed to last only ten minutes. Twice McKinley's secretary, George Cortelyou, had scrubbed this event, arguing that it was dangerous. Twice the president had written it back into the schedule, saying: "No one would wish to hurt me."

Although Cortelyou dropped the subject, he made sure there was plenty of security. Eighteen exposition policemen and eleven well-armed soldiers formed a lane through which people passed to greet the president. Three Secret Service agents were also on hand.

The Secret Service had been organized by the Treasury Department in 1865 to investigate and prevent counterfeiting. It was not responsible for protecting the president but its agents helped with security on an informal basis. Unfortunately, the arrangements were so informal that no one was really in charge. Nor did the agency have any system to detect potential killers before they struck. One of these, a man named Leon Czolgosz (pronounced *chol-gosh*) entered the line of handshakers without the slightest difficulty.

Czolgosz, a native of Cleveland, had suffered a mental breakdown some years earlier. He drifted into anarchism, a philosophy that considered all rulers evil, and became obsessed with the assassination of the king of Italy in 1900 by an American-born anarchist. Czolgosz had been talking about killing McKinley ever since.

Incredibly, not one of the supposedly alert guards noticed

when Czolgosz, while standing in the receiving line, drew a pistol from his pocket and wrapped a handkerchief around it, making it look as if he were wearing a bandage on his right hand. By awful coincidence, the man just ahead of him had an authentic bandage on his right hand. When the man reached the president, he said: "Excuse my left hand, Mr. President." McKinley smiled and shook his left hand.

When Czolgosz approached the president, he, too, extended his left hand. As McKinley reached for it, the anarchist fired two shots through the handkerchief at point-blank range. The president toppled backward into the arms of those around him. Fatally wounded, he died eight days later.

The sad story almost speaks for itself. Today, the Secret Service would very likely have heard of Czolgosz before he even got to Buffalo. Assuming the killer made it that far, they never would have let him get away with his gun-wrapped-in-a-handkerchief ruse. Even the innocent man who preceded him would have been hustled off before he got anywhere near the president.

V

After the McKinley assassination, the Secret Service was put in charge of protecting the president and two agents were assigned full-time to the White House detail. Even then there were lapses.

Theodore Roosevelt often had evening appointments. Most of his callers were known in advance, but occasionally there were people whom the president had asked to stop by without bothering to add their names to his schedule.

One evening a man appeared in full evening dress, complete with top hat, and informed the usher on duty at the front door that he had an appointment with the president. The man was invited to step into the Red Room and another usher went upstairs to tell the president that Mr. John Smith was there to see him. Roosevelt could not recall making an appointment with Mr. Smith but he decided to see him anyway.

The president went downstairs and within minutes pressed the call bell that summoned Chief Usher Ike Hoover to the Red Room. When Hoover entered, Roosevelt walked over to him and said quietly, "Take this crank out of here."

The president quickly left the room by another door while the chief usher signaled for help. When the visitor was searched, he was found to be carrying a large-caliber pistol.

With the onset of the Great Depression in 1929, the White House became a magnet for people who blamed the president for the collapse of the nation's economy. Herbert Hoover was inundated with death threats, crank letters, and bizarre visitors.

As a result, forty to fifty men were assigned to the White House Police Force and two Secret Service men accompanied the president whenever he went out. When he traveled, the number of agents was increased to eight or ten and additional men were recruited from Secret Service field offices in the areas he was visiting. In addition, White House visitors were subjected to greater scrutiny. Briefcases, cameras, and women's purses had to be inspected before their owners were admitted and anyone carrying a package was forbidden to approach the president.

In spite of this extra effort, slipups still occurred. Franklin

D. Roosevelt's oldest son, Jimmy, tells a story that the Secret Service would rather forget. One night during World War II, he was home on leave and joined his parents at the White House for dinner. Afterward they watched a movie. When the lights came on, a neatly dressed young man, a complete stranger, was standing next to FDR.

Instead of brandishing a weapon, however, the interloper asked for the president's autograph. Somehow, apparently for a lark, he had gotten past the doormen and the Secret Service to penetrate the heart of the house. FDR gave him the autograph and the embarrassed Secret Service men escorted him to the door. You can be sure this breach of White House security never happened again.

VI

These days, there are an estimated two hundred agents assigned to the White House, although they are not all on duty at the same time. Other Secret Service agents protect such potential targets as the vice president, presidential and vice presidential candidates and nominees, former presidents and their spouses, and visiting heads of state. In addition, the Secret Service continues to investigate counterfeiting and other types of financial fraud.

The Secret Service agents assigned to the White House detail wear civilian clothes and operate from a command post under the Oval Office. Agents are stationed near the second-floor living area and at one of the doors leading to the Oval Office. At least one agent accompanies the president whenever he leaves the family quarters.

The Secret Service also has a Uniformed Division. Its officers are posted at strategic areas around the White House. One unit, wearing black combat gear and silver helmets, cruises the President's Park on multigear mountain bikes. Another, the Secret Service Counter-sniper Team, is stationed on the White House roof whenever protectees are entering or leaving the building or are anywhere on the grounds.

VII

Not a little of the Secret Service's commitment to presidential safety emanates from tall, strong-jawed Edmund Starling. He started his job at the White House in 1914. In the course of his career, he worked for, or with, Presidents Wilson, Harding, Coolidge, Hoover, and Roosevelt. In those days the government paid for practically nothing except the Secret Service man's gun. Starling and his fellow agents had to buy their own evening clothes so they could participate in White House receptions.

Probably because he looked so physically impressive, Starling was often mistaken for the president. One day, Starling and Calvin Coolidge were out for a walk near the White House not long after Warren Harding died and Coolidge had become yet another accidental president.

As they passed a gang of laborers digging a ditch, the Irish foreman spotted them and said to a Secret Service man a few feet ahead of them: "What a fine-looking fellow the new president is. So tall and straight! Who's the little fellow with him?"

The agent quietly informed the foreman that the little fellow was the president. "Glory be to God!" the Irishman said.

"Now ain't it a grand country when a wee man like that can get to be the grandest of them all?"

Like many presidents, Calvin Coolidge at first declined to take the Secret Service seriously, and was always trying to sneak out of the White House without them. Starling converted this habit into a game, which he invariably won. He asked the staff to let him know when the president was planning to leave the mansion and what exit he would take.

One day Coolidge was sure he had won. He had descended to the White House basement and slipped out a side door at the east entrance. As he passed the sentry box, Starling stepped out and said: "Good morning, Mr. President." Cal did not speak to him for the entire walk.

VIII

One of the largest units of the Secret Service's Washington office is its Technical Security Division, which provides security devices for the White House. The division has installed such low-tech protection as the fat concrete stanchions, called bollards, that line the sidewalks around the mansion, as well as such high-tech apparatus as the electronic locator boxes that indicate where their protectees are every minute of the day and night.

Among the other devices the division can take credit for are the hydraulic gates at the vehicular entrances, the video and alarm systems along the perimeter and the radioactivity detectors in the areas adjacent to the Oval Office to indicate the presence of any nuclear devices.

The Technical Security Division also handles packages and

letters addressed to the White House that might contain lethal substances. Packages can be X-rayed at a Secret Service examining room several blocks away from the White House where they are also tested for timing devices. If the thing ticks, it is immediately soaked in oil to gum up the machinery— a good reason not to send any president a watch or clock as a gift.

If the Secret Service has reason to suspect a package is deadly, it is placed in a special egg-shaped bomb carrier mounted on a truck that can withstand the blast of fifty sticks of dynamite. The package is then driven to a deserted area where a specially trained agent opens it with grappling hooks operated from outside the truck.

IX

Federal law provides Secret Service protection for presidential families, a mandate that has involved the agents in some unlikely assignments for brawny males trained to do battle with killers.

One of these family assignments still makes me chuckle every time I think of it. Two agents were ordered to protect Barbara Ann Eisenhower, President Eisenhower's twelve-year-old granddaughter, while she attended an all-girls camp in West Virginia. The agents lived in a tent next to Barbara Ann's and were soon participating in cookouts, campfires, and Indian dances. The twelve-year-olds were entranced to have these two proto-heroes in their midst. At the end of the summer they made them members of their sacred campers' club— the only males ever so honored.

The agents assigned to guard Lyndon Johnson's older daughter, Lynda Bird, encountered even more complications. She belonged to Zeta Tau Alpha at the University of Texas in Austin. The sorority house was in a large white colonial mansion near the campus. After some no doubt delicate negotiations, the Secret Service persuaded the Zeta Taus to allow two Secret Service agents into their all-female ménage. The guys operated out of a small first-floor room equipped with a closed-circuit TV system that enabled them to see everyone who entered the house. The room also contained a two-way radio and enough guns to hold off a small army.

Nowadays, the Secret Service has women in its ranks. With female agents, the job of guarding presidential daughters and granddaughters is a lot less sticky. But it doesn't have nearly as much potential for amusement.

X

In their efforts to keep the residents of the White House safe, the Secret Service is determined to leave nothing to chance. The thought of a president being attacked on home turf appalls them, which undoubtedly explains a story told to me by a recent visitor to the West Wing. While using the men's room, he noticed that the neatly folded paper hand towels were imprinted with "The President's House" and blithely pocketed a couple of them as souvenirs.

When he emerged, a Secret Service agent fell in step beside him and asked him to return the towels. There would be no charge, the agent added with a smile. It seems that the men's room is monitored by a two-way mirror to make sure no one decides to load a pistol or set the fuse of a bomb in there.

Some people may think this is carrying security a bit too far. But in and around the White House, eternal vigilance is the price of safety. At seven A.M. on December 6, 2001, the Secret Service arrested a twenty-six-year-old man "acting suspiciously" near the southwest gate. He was armed with a foot-long knife and when he led them to his pickup truck, they found an assault rifle, another rifle with a scope that snipers use to kill people at a distance, and a loaded handgun. The man, who had no fixed address, was jailed on weapons charges.

Such incidents, which barely get a paragraph in the newspapers, only underscore that being president of the United States is dangerous work. I am sure every member of a presidential family pauses now and then to thank God that the Secret Service is on the job. I do it regularly.

Questions for Discussion

1. Can a president ever be completely safe?

2. How might the history of the country have been different if the Secret Service had been guarding Abraham Lincoln?

3. How has modern technology helped the Secret Service do its job?

☆　☆　☆

Look at the line waiting to get into President William Howard Taft's 1911 New Year's reception. I'm glad I didn't have to shake hands with them all. Credit: Library of Congress

☆ 15 ☆

The People's White House

ONE EVENING PRESIDENT Franklin Pierce was strolling the White House grounds, enjoying music from the Marine Band and nodding cordially to hundreds of tourists and local Washingtonians. A man nervously approached him and said: "Mr. President, can't I go through your fine house? I've heard so much about it that I'd give a great deal to see it."

Pierce replied: "Why, my dear sir, that is not my house. It is the people's house! You shall certainly go through it if you wish." Summoning a doorman, he ordered the visitor to be given a thorough tour of the first-floor rooms.

That touching tale sums up one side of the story of tourists in the White House, a very important side. But the whole story is a lot more complicated. The first uninvited visitors appeared in the President's House in 1800, even before the place was finished. These unwanted callers became so numerous and so nosy, the commissioners in charge of the new capital's public buildings ordered them barred unless they had a written pass justifying their presence. This rule did not discourage numerous local ladies, who conned written passes out of friendly bureaucrats and were soon sashaying all over the house.

A tradition had been launched that future residents of the White House would sometimes cheer and sometimes lament. Whose house was it, anyway? The American people apparently thought it belonged to them. But presidential families would occasionally exclaim: "What about us? Don't we have a vote on that question?" Most of the time, the answer was no.

II

President Thomas Jefferson ordered the White House doors kept open every day, so visitors could inspect the State Rooms on the first floor. They were more interested in Jefferson's basement kitchen, which had a fireplace equipped with an iron range—very rare at the time. Jefferson also added what we would call tourist attractions. Lewis and Clark shipped skins of hitherto unknown beasts and birds from the west. Zebulon Pike and General James Wilkinson, commander of the U.S. Army, also sent their share of dinosaur bones and Indian artifacts from Texas and other unmapped portions of the southwest.

Pike's biggest contribution to the displays were two grizzly bear cubs. Jefferson put them in a ten-foot-square cage in the middle of the circular driveway on the north side of the White House. People came from miles around to get a look at these creatures. Eventually he had to ship them to Baltimore where presidential portrait painter Charles Willson Peale maintained a natural history museum, a forerunner of the modern zoo.

Some of Jefferson's tourists were even more exotic than the cubs. They arrived wearing feathered headdresses, deerskin moccasins, cloth leggings, and streaks of paint on their faces. The president had told Lewis and Clark to extend invitations to visit the "Great Chief" of the white men in Washington to any and all tribes they met along their route west. Jefferson probably did not realize that Indians were prodigious travelers, who loved an excuse for a journey. Soon chiefs from several western tribes were camping on the White House lawn, along with their squaws and their uncles and their cousins and their aunts.

III

The first president to curtail access to the White House was James Monroe. The few people who succeeded in getting in did not have much of a tour. The State Rooms were off limits and although the East Room may have impressed visitors by its size, it had little else going for it. There was no furniture and the chandeliers were drab metal.

Monroe's successor, John Quincy Adams, tried to overcome his lack of appeal to the voters by keeping the White House wide open all day, every day. Anyone could come in and wander around. If he wanted to shake the president's hand, all he had to do was join the line of callers waiting on the stairs.

On one occasion, Adams was the beneficiary of his open house policy. The president was conferring in his oval study with Secretary of State Henry Clay when one Eleazar Parraly strolled into the room. Parraly was mainly interested in shaking the president's hand, but in the course of introducing himself, he mentioned that he was a dentist. The president instantly dismissed the secretary of state and invited Parraly to remove a tooth that was aching ominously. There was no resident dentist in the national capital. Parraly not only did the job, he refused to take money for it.

IV

When President Andrew Jackson had the good fortune to receive a $50,000 appropriation from Congress to refurbish the White House, he spent a large chunk of it on finishing the magnificent cavern called the East Room. On the floor went a Brussels carpet, new draperies framed the windows, and three cut-glass chandeliers were suspended from the ceiling. New furniture was purchased and twenty spittoons were placed at strategic points around the room.

The rest of the house was not accessible to uninvited visitors. The White House grounds, however, were open from eight A.M. to sundown to anyone in the mood for a stroll. Enjoying the President's Park became popular and first families often grew more than a little discomfited when they glanced out the window and found twenty or thirty people staring up at them.

V

The Civil War made the White House even more fascinating to the American people. A good many of the tourists of those years were transported to Washington at government expense. They were wearing army blue, and the White House was only a way stop on their journey to fight and possibly die in Virginia. Lincoln gave orders to admit soldiers freely to the first floor, where they gaped at the East Room and occasionally stretched out on one of the sofas for a nap.

The rest of the first-floor rooms were closed to visitors. Concern for Lincoln's safety was one reason for not encouraging wanderers. Another reason was the visitors' tendency to carve souvenirs out of the rugs, draperies, and upholstery.

After Lincoln's assassination, the White House collapsed into near chaos. Mary Lincoln spent the next few weeks weeping and brooding in her upstairs bedroom, forcing the new president, Andrew Johnson, to set up his office in the Treasury Building next door. This left the President's House with no one in charge. It remained open to visitors and the public came pouring in. For most of each day, they swarmed through the State Rooms, collecting mementoes of the martyred president and wreaking havoc in the process.

Vases, lamps, and small statues vanished and still the pillagers were not satisfied. They proceeded to cut chunks out of the draperies and carpets. After they discovered the chest where the silver and china were stored, these items, too, disappeared at a dismaying rate.

VI

That orgy of misbehavior made everyone connected to the White House a lot more wary of tourists. It was generally recognized that some sort of supervision was needed. The Civil War had made Americans history-minded. The number of

Washington sightseers kept growing each year. The President's House was a place where they could glimpse the early days of the republic.

The mansion was redecorated after Andrew Johnson moved in and all evidence of vandalism was erased. Sightseers were again welcome to visit the East Room, but there were detectives on hand to make sure nothing was removed.

If the doorkeepers were not busy, one of them would double as a tour guide and spice up the visit with tidbits of White House history. Sightseers heard about Abigail Adams's wash hanging in the East Room, Andrew Jackson's chaotic inaugural reception, and the rebuilding of the White House after the British burned it down during the War of 1812.

The White House had achieved reverential status but that did not eliminate the souvenir hunters. On the contrary, it may even have stimulated them. The East Room was open to the public three days a week, and despite the presence of plainclothes detectives, there were always a few things missing when visiting hours ended. Even the select group of tourists who had special passes to visit the state parlors regularly indulged in petty thievery. According to Rutherford B. Hayes's son, Birch, "After every public reception a man had to go the rounds with a basket of crystal pendants to replace those taken from the chandeliers. They cut pieces off the bottoms of curtains and carried off everything in sight."

VII

When Theodore Roosevelt launched his vast White House redecoration and building program, public interest was intense. Pictures of the East Room, resplendent with ivory and gilt, filled the magazines and thousands came to see it with their own eyes. That was about all they saw. Roosevelt was not enthusiastic about tourists. His successor, William Howard Taft, was very much the opposite. During his administration, visitors were actually admitted to the Oval Office, and when the president was out of town they could bounce in Big Bill's chair.

Woodrow Wilson shared Theodore Roosevelt's attitude toward tourists but his daughters Margaret, Jessie, and Nellie found them a good source of laughs. Every once in a while they would join the crowd waiting to get into the White House and walk through the downstairs rooms, making catty remarks about themselves. "I wonder where that stuck-up creature Margaret Wilson is hiding today," Jessie would say.

"Yes," Nellie would reply. "I'd like to see her, just to give her hair a good yank. I hear she wears a wig."

The tourists around them would be horrified. Any minute they expected the White House police to arrest the entire crowd.

VIII

The flow of tourists ceased when Woodrow Wilson declared war in 1917, and did not resume until Warren Harding became president in 1921. Harding, having nothing better to do all day—his administration was run mainly by his cabinet and staff—began coming downstairs around lunchtime to greet the tourists. People liked it and soon crowds gathered to exchange a few words with the supposedly great man.

Calvin Coolidge felt no need to greet the tourists or anyone else, if he could help it. He shortened the visiting hours and let the ushers deal with the crowds. Herbert Hoover might have done the same thing if the stock market had not collapsed early in his presidency. With the country sinking into the Great Depression, Hoover decided visiting the White House might boost public morale. He ordered the mansion opened to visitors from ten A.M. to four P.M. every day except Sunday.

The president's sense that the people's house could serve as a beacon of hope during the dark days of the Depression was on target. People were eager to visit the mansion and the number of tourists doubled to 900,000 a year.

The flood of visitors continued when Franklin D. Roosevelt became president, and the White House grounds remained popular with tourists and Washingtonians out for a stroll. This free and easy access to the President's Park ended with the declaration of war against Japan on December 8, 1941, and it has never resumed. The White House, and the country, had lost its innocence.

IX

A lovely leftover from those bygone days is the annual lighting of the White House Christmas tree. In December 2001, after much internal debate, the Secret Service reversed its decision to bar everyone without a ticket to the ceremony because of their fear of a terrorist attack. It was heartening to know that the Secret Service had decided President George W. Bush could undertake this ceremony, which goes back to

1923. That year, Calvin Coolidge had gotten a letter from a Washington, D.C., public school janitor, suggesting it would be a nice idea to start the holiday season by lighting a tree on the South Lawn. Coolidge imported a balsam fir from his native Vermont and presidents have been performing this pleasant chore ever since. The ceremony was moved to the Ellipse in 1954.

At five P.M. on December 6, 2001, President Bush pushed a switch and ignited red, white, and blue lights on a forty-foot Colorado blue spruce. Soprano Audra McDonald and country singer Travis Tritt performed, starting a month-long pageant in which Washington-area dance groups and choirs appeared nightly. The symbolic blend of patriotism and the ancient feast of Christmas was hailed by everyone as a stirring reminder of what our soldiers were defending in the war against terrorism.

Another festive event that adds a unique dimension to the people's house is the annual Easter Monday egg rolling festival, which features folksingers, jugglers, and clowns in traditional regalia and in bunny costumes. The first lady is the official hostess of the event. The president blows a whistle and the kids, armed with spoons, start trying to persuade their hard-boiled eggs to roll across the sloping grass. In the end, the first lady declares everyone a winner and the children each get a wooden egg to take home as a souvenir. Not surprisingly, the Easter egg roll has become the largest public event of the White House year.

X

Visitors to the contemporary White House are unlikely to get a glimpse of the president, much less shake his hand and give him their thoughts about the economy. Yet that does not stop them from getting in touch with him in other ways. Faxes and E-mail have become increasingly popular, but letters remain the medium of choice for Mr. and Mrs. John Q. Citizen.

The American people have been sending letters to the White House since 1800. Some of our early presidents tried to read and answer these missives personally, but as the numbers increased, the chore was passed to a secretary. By the end of the nineteenth century, when even two secretaries were not enough to keep up with the flow, the mail room was created.

Its staff grew from one man—handling about a hundred letters a day in 1897—to twenty-two in the Truman era. Another fifty or so people were on a standby list for emergency days when, for various reasons, the letters and parcels leaped from an average of 8,000 a day to an avalanche of 150,000.

The current White House mail room, now called the Correspondence Office, has a staff of almost ninety people plus a couple of dozen interns and a pool of over seven hundred volunteers. Most correspondents receive some kind of reply, usually a printed card rather than a regular letter.

Letters that might be of special interest to the president are extracted from the pile and brought to his attention. President George H. W. Bush's staff secretary once sent a memo to the Correspondence Office stressing the importance of being on the lookout for such letters. Attached was a letter addressed to President Franklin D. Roosevelt telling him about a theory the writer had that could create an unbelievably powerful bomb. The letter was badly typed and full of misspellings and crossed-out words but an alert mail handler had rescued it from the "nut file" and sent it on to the president. It was signed: Albert Einstein.

XI

Another avenue to the president is the telephone. Many of the callers have questions, such as how to apply for veterans' benefits or what their Medicare coverage includes. The operators cannot answer such queries but they provide the callers with the phone numbers of the government agencies that can give them the information they need.

The line also attracts a fair number of mentally ill callers. Although their comments often make very little sense, these callers are treated with the same courtesy as everyone else. For threatening calls, there is a buzzer that connects the call to the Secret Service and they take it from there.

Comment line volunteers will not stay on the line forever, even though many people, both sane and insane, would like them to. They are instructed to limit the conversations to two minutes so other callers can get through.

XII

The Gift Office has been set up to deal with the approximately fifteen thousand gifts that arrive at the White House each year. A staff of about a half dozen highly experienced employees registers the gifts, sees that they are acknowledged, and decides what should be done with them. Many are gifts from foreign governments and are quite valuable. They are considered gifts to the nation rather than to the president and they are usually sent to the Smithsonian Institution or the Library of Congress or kept for use in a presidential library. The president is allowed to keep only those that have minimal value, which is currently defined as less than $260.

A high percentage of the gifts that arrive at the White House are sent by private citizens. If a president or a first lady has a special hobby or a fondness for a particular type of clothing, he or she is likely to get buried in the stuff. When Dad was seen pitching horseshoes on the White House lawn, horseshoes by the hundreds descended on us. A similar glut occurred when a reporter wrote a story about Caroline Kennedy's love of chocolate. The White House Gift Office logged in everything from Hershey bars to a 6-foot, 190-pound chocolate rabbit from Switzerland.

Jerry Ford once received—and kept—a hand-knitted ski hat that had been sent to him by a retired nun. After she spied him wearing it on a television news clip, she decided it looked too tight. She immediately sent him a letter with instructions on how to care for it: Wet it and let it sit on your head until it dries.

XIII

The White House is the only residence of a head of state in the entire world that can be visited by the public free of charge. Before the terrorist attacks of September 11, 2001, it was open Tuesday through Saturday from ten A.M. to 12 noon. This wonderful privilege was one of the many casualties of that dire day. Since then, the Secret Service has decreed that only limited public tours are permissible, and even these may be suspended in the event of a serious security threat.

A tour of the White House begins in the East Wing. Visitors pass through the ground floor corridor before ascending the staircase to view the historic rooms on the main floor. The corridor was a grubby work area until Charles McKim got his hands on it in 1902. He restored the vaulted ceiling and covered the walls and floors with marble. It is now a red-carpeted entrance worthy of welcoming the most exalted VIPs.

I have a special fondness for the rooms that open off the ground-floor corridor because their wood paneling was made from the timber that was removed from the White House during the Truman renovations. The Vermeil Room, which is used as a ladies' sitting room at formal events, features an exhibit of some rare pieces of vermeil—gilded silver. Next to it is the China Room, where items from the White House china collection are displayed and Howard Chandler Christy's portrait of Grace Coolidge dominates one wall. On the north side of the corridor is the library, which serves as a male counterpart to the ladies' sitting room across the hall. It's always a shock for me to realize that prior to the 1902 renovation, this beautiful space was a laundry room.

Upstairs, the East Room still features the Gilbert Stuart portrait of George Washington that Dolley Madison rescued from British torches so long ago. On the mantels of the west wall are exquisite golden bronze candelabra bought in France by Elizabeth Monroe in 1817. The Green Room, completely redone by First Lady Pat Nixon in 1971, is still a treasure trove of Federal period furniture. The furnishings also include Gilbert Stuart's wonderful portraits of President John Quincy Adams and First Lady Louisa Catherine Adams.

The Blue Room, refurbished by Hillary Clinton in 1995, has seven of the gilded chairs Elizabeth Monroe purchased from one of Paris's foremost cabinetmakers. The rest of the furniture is in the same elegant Empire style. The mahogany marble-top table is one of the oldest pieces of furniture in continuous residence; it was bought by the Monroes in 1817 and has never left the mansion.

The Red Room is also in the Empire style. During the 1840s, this was called the Washington Room because Stuart's portrait of the ultimate Founding Father resided here. Another Gilbert Stuart portrait, this one of Dolley Madison, is one of the room's highlights. Dolley still emanates the marvelous good cheer that made her supreme.

The State Dining Room is almost as impressive as the East Room. Enlarged over the years, it can now seat 140 people comfortably. Above the mantel hangs George P. A. Healy's portrait of Abraham Lincoln, gazing down at the nation he preserved. He's all by himself on these walls—a lonely splendor that no one will ever contest.

That's a small sample of what you'll see in the President's House when you visit during the hours when it is also the people's house.

Questions for Discussion

1. How have historic events influenced public attitudes toward the White House?

2. Why did it become necessary to restrict access to the White House?

3. What do you consider the most interesting room in the White House and why?

The entrance hall at the North Portico has witnessed over two hundred years of history. Let's hope there are hundreds more to come. Credit: White House Historical Association

The White House Forever

A HUNDRED YEARS from now, if another presidential daughter walks by the White House in the twilight, what will she see and think? I am prepared to bet a large sum that it will be the same glowing vision, igniting different memories but invoking essentially the same experience. She will wonder how she survived it—and at the same time feel a wry mingling of gratitude.

By that time, the walls of the old house may be lined with titanium to withstand terrorist attacks, and the Secret Service may have equipment that enables them to do everything but read the minds of visitors. But the staff will still be smiling and undaunted by any and all presidential requests. Children will still play in the upstairs halls and pets will romp on the South Lawn. The West Wing will be as full of devoted, energetic staffers as it is today and the media will still be tormenting presidents and press secretaries with nosy questions. Diplomats and VIPs will mingle at receptions and state dinners. The first lady will preside in the East Wing, continuing the White

House tradition of graciousness and good taste and perhaps exerting some womanpower along the way—that is, unless there is a first man, trying to carve out a new role for presidential spouses. The president will prowl the halls at night, studying the faces of his—or her—predecessors on the walls.

Most important, the American people will remain fascinated by the President's House. It will continue to be not only the most beautiful public building in Washington, but a living museum of the nation's history. The mansion's story will recall the triumphs and tragedies of the United States of America and its chosen leaders. At the heart of the story will be the underlying idea everyone who lives or works there senses: glory. I still feel it every time I walk into 1600 Pennsylvania Avenue. I hope this book has brought some of it alive for you.

Index

Page numbers in *italics* refer to illustrations.

Adams, Abigail, 19, 65, 118, 120, 252
Adams, John, 19, 65, 72, 212
Adams, John Quincy, 9, 36–37, 43, 86,
    139–40, 213, 249, 260
Adams, Louisa Catherine, 86, 139–40,
    260
aides, 97–111
Amen, Marion Cleveland, 156
Appointments Lobby, 97
Arlington National Cemetery, 161,
    229

Bennett, James Gordon, 213–14
Bill of Rights, 211–12
Birdzell, Donald T., 230, 231
Bizet, Charles, 36
Blair, Francis Preston, 212
Blair House, 29, 212, 229
Blue Room, 20, 26, 85, 173, 181, 260
Boettiger, Anna, 143
Booth, John Wilkes, 54
Bosanquet, Esther Cleveland, 134,
    155–56
brides, *170*, 171–88
Bruce, Preston, 129
Bryant, Traphes, 204–5
Buchanan, James, 40, 88, 99
Bundy, McGeorge, 57
Bush, Barbara, 127, 206

Bush, George H.W., 44, 206, 224, 256
Bush, George W., 111, 167, 197, 224,
    254–55
Bush, Jenna and Barbara, 166–67, 206
Bush, Laura, 167
butlers, 78–79, 129–30
Butt, Archie, 101–3

Cabinet Room, 57, 97
Camp David, 186, 187
Capitol, 23
Carter, Amy, 196
Carter, Jimmy, 196, 223–24
Carter, Rosalyn, 91, 196
Casals, Pablo, 7
Castro, Fidel, 57
Central Intelligence Agency (CIA), 59
Chiang Kai-shek, Madame, 142–43
chief usher, 115–16, 142–43, 237
children, 150–68, 263
    Clinton, 166, 167
    Coolidge, 164–65
    Grant, 158–60
    Kennedy, 152–55
    Lincoln, 157–58
    Roosevelt, *150*, 161–64
    Secret Service and, 151, 241–42
Children's Garden, *34*, 45–46
China, 142, 175

China Room, 259
Christmas, 138, 153–54, 254–55
Christy, Howard Chandler, 204
Churchill, Winston, 7, 105, 137–39, 207, 219
Civil War, 22, 52, 53, 88, 161, 214–15, 233–34, 250–51
Clay, Henry, 86, 249
Cleveland, Frances Folsom, 89, 155, 173–74
Cleveland, Grover, 11, 41, 76, 101, 152, 155–56
  children of, 155–56
  media and, 215–16
  wedding of, 172–73
Cleveland, Rose, 89
Cleveland, Ruth, 155
Clifford, Clark, 108
Clinton, Bill, 44, 75, 77, 92, 166
  media and, 224
  pets of, 197
  staff, 110
Clinton, Chelsea, 166, 167
Clinton, Hillary Rodham, 44, 77, 166, 197, 260
  health care plan, 91–92
coffees and teas, 65, 77–78
Collazo, Oscar, 229–31
Color Team, 68, 196, 204
Comment Line office, 257
Commission of Fine Arts, 28
Congress, 5, 8, 10, 30, 59, 65, 66, 86, 90, 92, 118, 120, 161, 220–21
Connelly, Matt, 96, 107
Constitution, 119, 211–12
Coolidge, Calvin, 76, 119, 124–25, 133, 196, 218, 228, 239–40, 254, 255
  children of, 164–65
  pets of, 200–1, 203–4
Coolidge, Calvin, Jr., 164–65
Coolidge, Grace, 9, 204, 259
Coolidge, John, 164
Correspondence Office, 256
Cortelyou, George, 235
Cox, Edward, 185, 186
Cox, Tricia Nixon, 121, 129, 185–87

Crim, Howell, 142
Cuban missile crisis, 57–58
Currie, Betty, 197
Czolgosz, Leon, 235–36

Daniel, Clifton, 68, 222
Davis, Jefferson, 195
death threats and assassination attempts, 229–31
Declaration of Independence, 51
Democratic-Republicans, 18
DePriest, Mrs. Oscar, 140
dinners. see receptions and dinners
Diplomatic Reception Room, 56, 60
Donelson, Emily, 87
doormen, 122–23, 129, 252
Downing, Andrew Jackson, 39, 41

Early, Steve, 220
Easter egg roll, 161, 255
East Room, 24, 26, 54, 67, 71, 98, 157, 161, 162, 177, 184, 186, 222, 224, 249, 250, 252, 259
East Wing, 83, 259, 263
Edward VII, King of England, 89, 175
Einstein, Albert, 257
Eisenhower, Barbara Ann, 241
Eisenhower, David, 121, 185
Eisenhower, Dwight D., 4, 185, 193, 222, 241
Eisenhower, Julie Nixon, 48, 60, 121, 185
Eisenhower, Mamie, 135, 193
Elizabeth, Queen of England, 73, 132, 136
Elizabeth II, Queen of England, 44, 135
Ellipse, 41, 203, 255
Elliptical Saloon, 20, 85, 87
Emancipation Proclamation, 51–53
England, 36, 40, 136, 175
  War of 1812, 49–51
Evarts, William, 74
Executive Office Building, 25–26

families. see children; first ladies
Federal Bureau of Investigation (FBI), 59

Ficklin, Charles, 129
Ficklin, Samuel, 129
Fields, Alonzo, 78–79, 127, 130, 144
Fillmore, Millard, 9, 39
fire of 1814, 20, 51
first ladies, 83–93
  as campaigners, 86
  power of, 84–86, 90–93
  substitute, 87–89
  see also specific first ladies
Folsom, Oscar, 172
Ford, Betty, 60
Ford, Gerald, 6, 44, 60, 223, 231, 258
Fourth of July, 54–55, 75–77
furnishings, 9–10, 25, 30, 67, 133, 249,
  250, 259–60

gardens and grounds, 10, 17, 35–46
  Children's Garden, *34,* 45–46
  Fillmore, 39
  Jackson, 37–38
  Johnson, 45–46
  Kennedy, 44–45
  Olmstead, 43
  Roosevelt, 42
  Rose Garden, 26, 43, 44–45
  Wilson, 43, 45
Garfield, James A., 160, 215, 234
George VI, King of England, *132,* 136
Germany, 136, 138
ghosts, 12
Gift Office, 257–58
gifts, 69, 257–58
  wedding, 174–75, 179
Globe, 212
Grand Staircase, 68, 174
Grant, Buck, 158
Grant, Fred, 158
Grant, Jesse, 158, 159–60, 193
Grant, Julia, 158–59, 215
Grant, Ulysses S., 40–41, 119, 193–94,
  202, 215
  children of, 158–60, 176–77
Great Depression, 55, 76, 219, 237, 254
greenhouses, 25, 37, 40, 42
Green Room, 29, 259–60

guests and guest rooms, 133–47
  of FDR, *132,* 134, 136–39, 142–45
  royalty, *132,* 135, 142, 145

"Hail to the Chief," 7, 73
Haldeman, H.R., 122
Hamilton, George, 184
handshaking, 75, 76
Harding, Warren G., 164, 191, 239, 253
Harrison, Benjamin, 22, 41, 117,
  199–200, 234
Harrison, Caroline, 22
Harrison, William Henry, 11
Hay, John, 99–100, 111, 135
Hayes, Fanny, 160
Hayes, Lucy Webb, 73–74, 160–61, 162
Hayes, Rutherford B., 41, 43, 73–74,
  160–61, 199, 252
Hayes, Scott, 160–61
Henry, Buck, 99
history, 11, 49–61
Hoban, James, 18, 21, 26, 29, 31
Hoover, Herbert, 76, 98, 104, 118, 121,
  141, 145–47, 192, 203, 237, 239,
  254
Hoover, Ike, 117–18, 237
Hoover, Lou, 78, 118, 121, 141, 145–46,
  156
Hopkins, Harry, 104, 143
household staff, *114,* 115–30, 137–38,
  183
  slaves as, 118–119
  transition from one administration to
    the next, 120–22
housekeepers, 124–26
Howe, Louis, 134

Inauguration Day, 120
Internet, 224
Italy, 235

Jackson, Andrew, 9, 12, 21, 37–38, 39,
  51, 70–71, 86, 87, 118, 162, 202,
  212, 250, 252
Jackson magnolia, 35, 37, 44
Jaffray, Elizabeth, 119, 124

Japan, 195
Jefferson, Thomas, 18, 19–20, 25, 36, 41,
     54–55, 72, 76, 83, 98–99, 118, 212,
     231–32
   attitude toward women, 83–84
   tourism and, 247–48
Johnson, Andrew, 215, 234, 251, 252
Johnson, Lady Bird, 34, 45, 66, 181
Johnson, Lyndon B., 13–14, 66, 77,
     115–17, 166
   children of, 181–85
   pets of, 191, 205–6

Kennedy, Caroline, 152–55, 191, 194,
     198, 258
Kennedy, Jacqueline, 9, 45, 194
   children of, 152–55
   redecorating and entertaining, 30,
     68–69
Kennedy, John F., 44–45, 135
   assassination of, 66, 155, 181
   children of, 152–55
   Cuban missile crisis, 57–58
   media and, 222–23
   pets of, 192, 194, 198
   staff, 57, 109
Kennedy, John F., Jr., 152–55
Key, Francis Scott, 51
Khrushchev, Nikita, 194
Kissinger, Henry, 60
kitchen, 68, 121

Lafayette, Marquis de, 139–40
Lafayette Square, 39
La Guardia, Fiorello, 90
Lamont, Daniel, 101, 215
Lane, Harriet, 40, 88–89
League of Nations, 5
Lee, Robert E., 52, 53, 234
LeHand, Marguerite "Missy," 105
L'Enfant, Pierre Charles, 17–18, 23
letters to the president, 256–57
Lewis, Meriwether, 55, 98–99
Lewis and Clark, 55, 248, 249
library, 259

Lincoln, Abraham, 12, 51–53, 99–100,
     111, 123, 133, 199, 251, 260
   assassination of, 54, 123, 234, 251
   children of, 157–58
   death threats, 232–33
   media and, 215
Lincoln, Evelyn, 109
Lincoln, Mary, 52, 54, 133, 158, 233, 251
Lincoln, Tad, 123, 157, 199
Lincoln, Willie, 100, 157, 199
Lincoln Bedroom, 25, 51, 58, 133–34,
     139, 144
Lincoln Sitting Room, 58–59
Long, Ava, 78
Longworth, Alice Roosevelt, 134, 150,
     161, 164, 202
   wedding of, 174–76
Longworth, Nick, 174–75
López-Portillo, José, 196
Louisiana Purchase, 54–55
luncheons, 65, 77, 78

Madison, Dolley, 20, 50–51, 82, 84–85,
     87, 92, 259, 260
Madison, James, 20, 50, 84, 211, 232
Maher, Jemmy, 37
Marine Band, U.S., 7, 60, 66–67, 68,
     72–73, 76, 89, 173, 180, 196, 247
McAdoo, Nellie Wilson, 178,
     180–81
McAdoo, William Gibbs, 180
McKee, Benjamin Harrison, 199–200
McKim, Charles, 24–25, 42, 56, 216, 259
McKim, Eddie, 13
McKinley, Ida, 41
McKinley, William, 24, 41–42, 216
   assassination of, 234–36
McMillan Plan, 23–24
media, 6, 9, 56, 93, 101, 107, 146, 152,
     167, 187, 210, 211–25
   Cleveland and, 215–16
   Clinton and, 224
   Kennedy and, 222–23
   Lincoln and, 215
   pressroom renovations, 220–21

Reagan and, *210,* 224
Roosevelts and, 216–17, 218–20, 223
Truman and, 220, 221–22
see also radio addresses; *specific publications;* television
Merry, Anthony and Elizabeth, 84
Mexico, 196
military aides, 72, 175
Monroe, Elizabeth, 21, 259
Monroe, James, 21, 36, 76, 86, 139, 232, 249
Moton, Dr. Robert R., 141
Muffler, Johnny, 129

Napoleon Bonaparte, 54
National Intelligencer, 212
Native Americans, 7, 161, 249
Nesbitt, Henrietta, 125–26, 136
Nevin, Blanche, 178
New Year's Day, 75–76
New York *Herald,* 214
New York Times, 91
Nicolay, John George, 99–100, 111, 135
Nixon, Pat, 30, 59–60, 121, 259
Nixon, Richard M., 30, 116, 121, 122, 185–87, 220–21, 223
  resignation, 48, 58–60
Norman, Jessye, 7
North Portico, 21, 44, 124, 163, 196, 200, 211, 216, *262*
Nugent, Luci Johnson, 171, 181–83, 205
Nugent, Patrick, 182, 205

Office of Civilian Defense, 90
Ogle, Charles, 10–11
Olmstead, Frederick Law, Jr., 43
Ousley, John, 36, 38
Oval Office, 26, 43, 46, 59, 97, 101, 110, 146, 192, 198, 201, *210,* 220, 229, 238, 240, 253

paintings, 50–51, 259
Parks, Lillian Rogers, 4, 12
Pebble Beach, 211, 221
Pendel, Thomas, 123

Pentagon, 49
Perry, Commodore Matthew C., 195
pets, 157, *190,* 191–208
  Clinton, 197
  Coolidge, 200–1, 203–4
  Johnson, 191, 205–6
  Kennedy, 192, 194, 198
  Lincoln, 199
  Roosevelt, *190,* 192, 195, 198–99, 201, 207–8
Pfister, Henry, 42
phone calls, 257
Pierce, Franklin, 195, 214, 247
policemen, 230–31, 233, 237
Polk, James, 41, 69, 214
Polk, Sarah, 69
power, 13–14
  women, 84–93
press conferences, 218
press secretaries, 5, 107
Price, William, 216
Prince of Wales Room, 133
Prohibition, 78
protocol and etiquette, 68–69, 73–74

Queens' Bedroom, 134–35

racism, 118–119, 140–41, 220
radio addresses, 56, 218
Reagan, Ronald, *210,* 224, 231
receptions and dinners, 7, 20, 26–27, *64,* 65–79, 85, 122, 196, 263
Red Room, 20, 29, 176, 234, 237, 260
Reich, Robert, 110
religion, 58
renovation and redecoration, 9, 20–21, 250, 252–53
  Harrison, 22, 23
  Kennedy, 30
  McKim (1902), 24–25, 42, 83, 216, 259
  post-War of 1812, 29, 44, 220–21, 229, 252
  Truman, 27–30
Republican Party, 52

Revolutionary War, 139
Riley, Ellen, 124–25
Robb, Charles, 184
Robb, Lynda Bird Johnson, 171, 181,
    182, 183, 184–85, 242
Rogers, Maggie, 4
Roosevelt, Archie, 150, 162, 191,
    198–99
Roosevelt, Edith, 24–25, 42, 75, 202
Roosevelt, Eleanor, 77–78, 90, 93, 119,
    121, 125, 137, 143, 208
    media and, 219–20
Roosevelt, Ethel, 150, 162
Roosevelt, Franklin D., 10, 26, 35, 43,
    55–56, 78, 83, 90, 121, 125–26,
    237–38, 239, 254
    death of, 207, 220
    fireside chats, 56
    guests of, 132, 134, 136–39, 142–45
    media and, 218–19, 223
    pets of, 190, 192, 207–8
    staff, 104–6
Roosevelt, Kermit, 150, 162, 201
Roosevelt, Quentin, 150, 162–63, 198,
    201
Roosevelt, Theodore, 24–25, 42, 72,
    101–2, 133, 140–41, 150, 166, 175,
    236–37, 252–53
    children of, 150, 161–64, 174–76
    media and, 216–17
    pets of, 195, 198, 201
Roosevelt, Theodore, Jr., 150, 162
Rose Bedroom, 135, 137
Rose Garden, 26, 43, 44–45, 185, 186
Ross, Charlie, 5, 107, 167
Rove, Karl, 111
Royall, Anne, 213
Russia, 57–58, 74, 194

Salinger, Pierre, 191
Sartoris, Algernon, 176–77
Sartoris, Nellie Grant, 158, 170,
    176–77
Sayre, Frank, 178–80
Sayre, Jessie Wilson, 179–80
secretaries, 98–99

Secret Service, 4–5, 27, 49, 151, 228,
    229–43, 254, 257
    beginnings of, 235
    death threats and assassination
        attempts, 229–31
    protection for presidential families,
        241–42
    Technical Security Division, 240–41
    Uniformed Division, 239
segregation, 119, 220
September 11 terrorist attacks, 8, 49
Seward, William, 52, 53
Sinatra, Frank, 7
Situation Room, 17
slaves, 4, 51–53
    as White House staff, 118–119
Smith, Merriman, 98
social events, 7, 20, 26, 64, 65–79, 85
    handshaking, 75, 76
    Hayes, 73–74
    Jackson, 70–71, 87
    Kennedy, 68–69
    Marine Band at, 72–73
    protocol and etiquette, 68–69, 73–74
    Roosevelt, 72, 77–78
    royal visits, 73–74, 135–36, 142, 145
    Taft, 69–70
    weddings, 170, 171–88
South Portico, 2, 21, 44, 138
    Truman balcony, 9, 27–28
Soviet Union. see Russia
Spanish-American War, 216
staff, 97–130
    household, 114, 115–30, 137–38, 183
    West Wing, 96, 97–111
Stalin, Joseph, 105, 219
Stanton, Edwin, 100
Starling, Edmund, 228, 239
State Department, 143
State Dining Room, 20, 24, 28, 64, 67,
    74, 85, 114, 140, 173, 174, 177, 260
State Rooms. see specific rooms
Stephanopoulos, George, 110
Streisand, Barbra, 7
Stuart, Gilbert, 259, 260
Supreme Court, U.S., 59

Taft, Helen, 119, 124
Taft, William Howard, 4, 25–26, 69–70, 101–3, 117, 124, 203, 253
Taylor, Zachary, 39, 118, 202
telegraph, invention of, 214–15
television, 222
temperance, 73–74
"The Star-Spangled Banner," 51
Thomas, George, 128
Thomas, Helen, 6, 191, 224–25
Thompson, Herman, 128
Titanic, 103
Tito, Josip Broz, 154
Torresola, Griselio, 230–31
tourism, *246*, 247–60
  Christmas, 254–55
  curtailed, 8, 249, 254, 258–59
  Easter, 255
  garden tours, 46
  souvenir hunters, 251, 252
  tours, 259–60
trial balloons, 217
Truman, Bess Wallace, 26, 75, 92–93, 126, 134, 188, 231
Truman, Harry S, 5, 12, 13, 26–30, 31, 35, 44, 61, 67, 73, 75, 106, 119–20, 126, 128, 134, 152, 168, 171, 188, 193, 258
  assassination attempts against, 229–31
  media and, 220, 221–22
  staff, 107–8
Truman balcony, 9, 27–28, 154
Tumulty, Joseph, 103–4

Untiedt, Bryan, 145–47

Van Buren, Angelica, 87–88
Van Buren, Martin, 10–11, 76–77, 87, 214
Vermeil Room, 259

Wallace, Henry, 106
War of 1812, 20, 48, 49–51, 252
Washington, Booker T., 140

Washington, George, 10, 18–19, 31, 38, 50, 89, 212, 259
Washington Evening Star, 216
Watergate, 59, 223
Watson, Pa, 106
Watt, John, 40
weddings, *170*, 171–88
West, J.B., 115–16, 135
West Wing, 25, 26, 57, 229
  renovations, 216, 220–21
  staff, 97–111
Whigs, 9
White House
  brides and weddings, *170*, 171–88
  children, 151–68
  early design and building, *16*, 17–18
  first ladies, 83–93
  gardens and grounds, 35–46
  guests, 133–47
  history, 49–61
  household staff, 115–30
  media, 211–25
  pets, 191–208
  renovations and reconstructions, 20–21
  Secret Service, 229–43
  tourism, *246*, 247–60
  West Wing staff, 97–111
  see also specific rooms
White House Correspondents Association, 218
Wilson, Edith Galt, 104, 181
Wilson, Ellen, 26, 42–43, 45, 178–79, 181
Wilson, Margaret, 178, 253
Wilson, Woodrow, 5, 26, 42, 103–4, 120, 171, 239
  children of, 178–81, 253
  media and, 217–18
Works Progress Administration (WPA), 104–5
World War I, 253
World War II, 45, 61, 76, 83, 105, 138, 142, 219, 238, 254

© Clifton Daniel

MARGARET TRUMAN won faithful readers with her works of biography and fiction, particularly her ongoing series of Capital Crimes mysteries. Her novels let us into the corridors of power and privilege, and poverty and pageantry, in the nation's capital. She was the author of many nonfiction books, including *The President's House*, in which she shares some of the secrets and history of the White House where she once resided. She lived in Manhattan and passed away in 2008.

Printed in the United States
by Baker & Taylor Publisher Services